AVID
READER
PRESS

Spirit Daughter

OWN YOUR POWER, CHANGE YOUR LIFE

Jill Wintersteen

AVID READER PRESS

New York   Amsterdam/Antwerp   London
Toronto   Sydney/Melbourne   New Delhi

AVID READER PRESS
An Imprint of Simon & Schuster, LLC
1230 Avenue of the Americas
New York, NY 10020

For more than 100 years, Simon & Schuster has championed authors and the stories they create. By respecting the copyright of an author's intellectual property, you enable Simon & Schuster and the author to continue publishing exceptional books for years to come. We thank you for supporting the author's copyright by purchasing an authorized edition of this book.

No amount of this book may be reproduced or stored in any format, nor may it be uploaded to any website, database, language-learning model, or other repository, retrieval, or artificial intelligence system without express permission. All rights reserved. Inquiries may be directed to Simon & Schuster, 1230 Avenue of the Americas, New York, NY 10020 or permissions@simonandschuster.com.

Copyright © 2026 by Jill Wintersteen and Spirit Daughter, Inc.

All rights reserved, including the right to reproduce this book or portions thereof in any form whatsoever. For information, address Avid Reader Press Subsidiary Rights Department, 1230 Avenue of the Americas, New York, NY 10020.

First Avid Reader Press hardcover edition March 2026

AVID READER PRESS and colophon are trademarks of Simon & Schuster, LLC

Simon & Schuster strongly believes in freedom of expression and stands against censorship in all its forms. For more information, visit BooksBelong.com.

For information about special discounts for bulk purchases, please contact Simon & Schuster Special Sales at 1-866-506-1949 or business@simonandschuster.com.

The Simon & Schuster Speakers Bureau can bring authors to your live event. For more information or to book an event contact the Simon & Schuster Speakers Bureau at 1-866-248-3049 or visit our website at www.simonspeakers.com.

Interior design by Milly McKinnish

Manufactured in the United States of America

1 3 5 7 9 10 8 6 4 2

Library of Congress Control Number: 2025944825

ISBN 978-1-6680-7582-1
ISBN 978-1-6680-7584-5 (ebook)

Let's stay in touch! Scan here to get book recommendations, exclusive offers, and more delivered to your inbox.

To Michael McGuffin, without you this book and Spirit Daughter would not exist. Thank you for your wise words, amazing meals, and generous heart. I will love you always. May you be happy, may you be healthy, may you be free.

CONTENTS

CHAPTER ONE Remember Who You Are — 1

CHAPTER TWO We're All Asleep Until We're Not — 9

CHAPTER THREE Your Intuition Is Speaking — 19

CHAPTER FOUR Finding Magic — 39

CHAPTER FIVE Be Very, Very Still — 57

CHAPTER SIX The Comfort Zones That Rule Our Lives — 77

CHAPTER SEVEN It's All Part of the Process — 91

CHAPTER EIGHT The Dark Night — 105

CHAPTER NINE Go Where You Feel Good — 119

CHAPTER TEN The Heart Wants What It Wants — 133

CHAPTER ELEVEN Pain Is Inevitable, Suffering Is Optional — 149

CHAPTER TWELVE In This Moment, You Are Okay — 163

CHAPTER THIRTEEN Forgiveness Is Freedom — 173

CHAPTER FOURTEEN Learning to Trust Life Again — 183

CHAPTER FIFTEEN You Are the Light — 199

CHAPTER SIXTEEN Welcome Home — 211

CHAPTER SEVENTEEN You Choose It All — 221

CHAPTER EIGHTEEN You Can Have It All — 233

Acknowledgments — 243

Chapter One
REMEMBER WHO YOU ARE

Welcome.

If you landed here, you're in the right place. I've always found that books make their way into my hands just when I need them. I'm sure this book has landed with you because you are ready.

Maybe you know me as Spirit Daughter, my online persona. Perhaps you have no idea who I am and just stumbled upon this book, and it spoke to you. No matter how you found me, in the pages of this book, I'd like you to think of me as just Jill. I'm not a celebrity, I'm not a spiritual guru, nor do I have the answers to all of life's questions. I'm just Jill.

I'm just like you. I'm not connected by some special force to the Universe, and I'm certainly not enlightened. I have challenges and struggles. I have insecurities, issues around worthiness, and self-doubt. I have yet to meditate away my anxieties, and I probably have another decade of therapy ahead of me because, without it, I'm a mess.

The lessons in this book were born from necessity, an unlikely journey that took me from academic researcher in neuroscience to someone who was under federal investigation to the founder of an incredible online community where I empower people to live their best possible lives. I didn't come to understand everything I share from a theoretical standpoint. I learned it for survival. Every tool, every practice, every understanding came from the deep desire to save myself and the unproven confidence that I could do it.

The most dangerous lie we tell ourselves is that someone else or something outside of ourselves is going to save us. You can have any life you choose, but it's not going to be handed to you by the Universe, some mythical figure, or a stranger on the street. The truth is you are the only one who can save yourself. More importantly, you have the power to create a life that is filled with absolutely everything you desire, a life filled with meaning, connection, abundance, and love.

Your real power—the power that will change your life and enable you to manifest everything you desire—often appears when things fall apart. In our darkest hours, we must rely on ourselves and believe that our inner magic will give us what we need to transform and evolve.

In its final stages of development, as the butterfly struggles to squeeze out of the narrow passage of its cocoon, fluid is forced into its wings, strengthening them and preparing them to fly. Without that specific struggle, the butterfly's wings would remain soft, shriveled, useless. It might emerge with help, but it would never, ever fly.

If someone were to "save" the butterfly by cutting it out of its cocoon and helping it to avoid the struggle, it would never soar through the air living its fullest life.

The butterfly reminds you that the struggles, challenges, and pressures of your life aren't something you merely need to survive or overcome. And they aren't something you need to be saved from. They are exactly what your soul needs to find its power.

During moments of struggle, you must trust yourself and your intuition, more than you ever have before. The power required is already inside you, waiting to be discovered, waiting to save you, waiting to create the life you deserve and were born to live.

I want you to take in one truth and let it guide your entire life:

You are amazing.

Take that in and feel that statement like it's the truest thing you've ever heard.

You are made of the same substances that make up all the stars, the sun, and the Earth. You are the past, present, and future combined. You are home to a trillion cells, each operating in a beautiful dance together to give you the greatest gift of any being: consciousness. And with this consciousness, you can direct your intention to evolution, healing, and anything else you decide. You are in control of your life, no one else.

While this may sometimes feel scary because you are ultimately in charge of the life you live and accountable for it, it's also equally exciting because you have built-in mechanisms like intuition that can help you focus your conscious mind on whatever it is you want to create. You have the power to manifest any vision. And you have the power to focus your brain in such a way that it will accomplish anything.

Right now, as you read these words, you're likely aware of several things at once—the book in front of you, the sounds around you, perhaps a persistent worry about tomorrow's meeting or a lingering memory of something that happened yesterday. You might be experiencing one or two of the many emotions humans can feel, all while your body performs an untold number of complex tasks without you having to think about them. This awareness, this consciousness, is part of your power. But there's so much more to you than what you're currently aware of. The human soul is astonishing in its depth, complexity, and potential.

There exist layers upon layers of wisdom, creativity, and strength just beneath the surface of our everyday awareness.

And yet . . . most of us have forgotten our amazingness. We've become disconnected from this deeper knowing, this inherent power that resides within each of us and that gets lost in the demands of life. I had certainly forgotten my power and who I was at my core. I spent years in academia, believing power came from external validation, from degrees, achievements, and carefully constructed plans. I believed if I could just figure everything out, if I could control all the variables, then I would finally feel powerful. Then I would finally feel worthy of power.

When you forget your amazingness, when you disconnect from this innate power, you doubt, limit, or even sabotage yourself. You feel you're not good enough for relationships, promotions, or unconditional self-love. You look outside of yourself for a savior and end up giving your power and authority away to someone else. You end up waiting for some magical thing to change your life. When this doesn't come to pass, you're left feeling helpless, disconnected from your true power, your core essence. You then end up living a life that feels out of alignment with your soul because it is.

I've seen this misalignment in so many people. In the yoga students who came to my classes seeking peace but didn't believe they deserved it. In the millions of followers who resonate with my words but struggle to believe them for themselves. In my own journey, when I catch myself slipping back into old patterns of doubting my inner wisdom.

I felt this type of soul misalignment deeply during my years in academia, that constant sense of swimming upstream, of trying to force myself into a life that looked perfect on paper but left me feeling hollow inside. I remember the exact moment my misalignment became too loud to ignore. I was sitting in a basement lab at Johns Hopkins University, surrounded by data and research papers, everything I thought

I wanted, when a simple truth hit me: I couldn't breathe. Not in the physical sense, but in that soul-deep way that tells you something has to change. It wasn't dramatic. There was no crisis, no external reason to change course. Just that quiet but persistent knowing that I was living someone else's version of power and brilliance, not my own.

During my time in neuroscience, I learned that we're biologically set up to forget our brilliance. Our brains are processing an incredible amount of information at any given moment. Our eyes alone take in an estimated ten million bits of information per second, but our conscious mind only processes around forty bits. We filter out the rest, and along with it, often filter out our own power.

This filtering process, developed over thousands of years of human evolution, was originally meant to help us survive. Our hunter-gatherer ancestors needed to focus on immediate threats; they couldn't afford to contemplate their infinite potential while being chased by predators. Our brains evolved to filter out anything that wasn't essential for immediate survival. Unfortunately, our amazingness often gets filtered out along with everything else.

When was the last time you were fully aware of how incredible your body is, operating millions of complex processes every second without you having to think about them? When did you last marvel at your ability to imagine entire worlds in your mind? When did you last feel connected to the same force that moves planets and creates stars?

Your brain and body are astonishing. They are designed with perfection, and your brain is capable of so much more than you'll ever realize. It's doing so many things beyond the surface of your consciousness that it would, quite literally, blow your mind if you were aware of all its tasks. Evolution has helped us filter out most stimuli so that we can focus on the primary task in front of us, and our brain is especially attuned to threats—not big visions. But we're not living in the wild, afraid of saber-toothed tigers preying on us. Our brain, though, is still set up as if we were.

We can choose instead to program our brain's filter and tell it what to pay attention to. And how do we do this? Through intention-setting and taking conscious control over our attention. This is the key to directing our energy, our consciousness, and our brain. That's why it's at the heart of every manifestation technique I've ever taught.

When we set clear intentions, we tell our brain what's important. We direct our attention to choose what to allow past the filter. While our brain will still allow us to perceive only a small percentage of what's around us, we can program our filter to be attuned to experiences that align with our visions instead of experiences that reinforce our limiting beliefs. Your ability to tell your brain what's important to you and reprogram your filter to allow those things into your consciousness is part of your brilliance.

So why don't we use this brilliance? If we can program our brain to create any reality, why do we stay stuck in limiting patterns, failed relationships, or unfulfilling careers? Because we've forgotten this ability exists, we've forgotten our power.

This forgetting isn't permanent. The filters can be removed. The conditioning can be undone. The limiting beliefs can be broken and rearranged. Your amazingness isn't gone, it's just been hidden beneath layers of societal expectations, childhood programming, and biological filtering.

You have the opportunity this lifetime to break through these conditioned patterns that make you doubt yourself or forget your inherent brilliance. You have the power to shed any limiting belief, anything that doesn't belong to you, and awaken to the miracle of your mind and energy. You have the power to write your story.

The truth is, you've never actually lost your amazingness. You've simply forgotten where to look for it. It's always been there, lost in the sea of your to-do lists or busy life. It got lost when you gave your power away to the notion of success, expectations, or someone else's beliefs about you. But once you step away from all the external noise and learn to see past the distractions, you'll find it. You'll find your amazingness. And even if you don't believe that right now, I'll believe for you. I believe in your amazingness.

In the chapters ahead, we'll explore how to remember this truth about yourself. We'll discover how to peel back the layers of your conditioning that block your power. I'll show you how to trust the wisdom that's always been within you. And, ultimately, you'll learn how to live from a place of knowing your own power. We'll also talk about how to intentionally focus the filter of your brain to manifest your life and take back any power you gave away to anyone else. Because once you remember who you really are, that's when the real journey begins.

Chapter Two
WE'RE ALL ASLEEP UNTIL WE'RE NOT

Often we begin a journey of awakening our power by recognizing that we landed in a life that feels unfulfilling. We may be in a job that doesn't make us happy, not have enough money to pay the bills, in a relationship that doesn't feel right, or stuck in an addictive pattern of avoidance. We might even begin this journey from rock bottom when we have no choice but to dig deep to get out.

Something clicks, though, and we wake up one day in a life that feels tense and misaligned. Even if we don't quite know what that means or how to change it—we recognize when we are unhappy. And that unhappiness creates a powerful motivator for change, once we recognize it and learn to break through the fog it often creates in our mind.

Misalignment is uncomfortable. It drains us and gives us a constant anxious feeling. Even when we can't describe how or why our life is misaligned, we feel it. Our intuition knows, our body knows, and our energy knows. Something is off and something greater is waiting. It may feel like a constant tension in your body, like you're trying to force every breath and something you desperately want is just out of reach.

When we're misaligned in our life, things may look good from the outside. We may get a great job, a promotion, a wedding ring, or the "perfect" home. We know well that so many people have a fabulous-looking life from the outside but are actually miserable on the inside. They may have focused their attention and manifestation power on a fancy job, a big home, or the perfect Instagram-worthy trips. That doesn't mean these manifestations are aligned with their soul.

Your brain is a humble servant of your visions. If you create a vision and focus your attention on it, it will manifest. Even if it's not aligned with who you really are and even if it will bring you unhappiness, your brain will create it if you tell it to.

This is why alignment matters. We can manifest a life that looks successful on the outside, but if that life is not filled with meaning and connections that open our hearts, we won't be happy. Even if our conscious mind decided that was the life it wanted to create, our deeper self always knows better and will illuminate our unhappiness until we wake up to it.

Many of us, myself included, end up living a life that doesn't bring connection and meaning. It may look great on paper and it may even be an example of how we can manifest anything. But if it's not aligned with our soul and doesn't bring us true joy, then it will ultimately end up feeling wrong.

This misalignment, though, is actually the beginning of awakening. The discomfort you feel when life doesn't fit quite right is not a sign that you're doing something wrong. It's your inner wisdom, your power, beginning to stir. Like a plant pushing through concrete, your truth will find its way to the surface, often in ways that feel like breaking.

I remember feeling the beginnings of my own misalignment in

graduate school. I had manifested a perfect journey for myself, one that looked great on paper and made everyone in my life proud. Heck, I was even proud of myself. I had accomplished a lot at a young age. But my journey, as excellent as it appeared, wasn't aligned with my soul. I felt tense, I felt anxious, I knew something wasn't quite right, and I found myself unable to make decisions that would move me forward because, subconsciously, I knew I wasn't moving in the direction of my soul.

Awakening to my misaligned academic life didn't come through a crisis, per se. It came through the gradual accumulation of moments that led me to realize I could no longer access the person I really was. I had lost touch with my core and sense of self. For some, this type of awakening does come through crisis, like a lost job, a failed marriage, or some other big event that wakes you out of your slumber. It could be a moment that forces you to reevaluate every choice you've ever made. Whether it's a moment of awakening or a slow burn, what feels like falling apart is actually, eventually, falling into alignment.

Think about a time when everything you thought you knew about yourself was challenged. Maybe it was a relationship ending that forced you to rediscover who you were. Maybe it was a career setback that made you question your path or even your future. Maybe it was simply waking up one day and realizing you couldn't keep living on autopilot. These moments of disruption—when everything feels most unstable—are our greatest invitations to remember our power.

The awakening process isn't always comfortable. In fact, it rarely is. When I first began to question my carefully planned path in academia, every external voice told me I was making a mistake. Society, family, colleagues—they all had opinions about what my life should look like. But somewhere beneath all that noise, my inner wisdom was becoming louder than my fear and I began to trust it.

At first, this trust feels impossible. When I first began listening to my inner wisdom, it seemed absurd. My logical mind had a field day listing all the reasons why abandoning my once-resounding yeses was disastrous. I wondered if I would ever be able to align my life or if I had the power to create a reality that felt good to me on every level. I wondered if I had the willpower to get through the challenging parts of leaving a well-planned, approved-by-society, and familiar life for the unknown.

Our default mode is to choose the familiar. Our brain is wired in a way that makes the familiar seem safe, protected, and comfortable. We are encouraged by our very DNA to choose situations that seem known. But that's not where our potential is and it's not where our power is. In order to align our life with who we really are and to align it with our full amazingness, we must be willing to leave our comfort zones of familiarity and leap into the unknown. This choice is scary, it goes against what our mind is trained to do, and it is the only way to a life aligned with our soul. Yes, there will always be struggle in the decision to leave a comfort zone, but remember it's the struggle that allows the butterfly to fly. It's the struggle that gives you the power to save yourself.

The first time you choose to trust your inner wisdom over external validation and comfort, it feels like stepping off a giant cliff. You have no idea what will happen next, where you will land, or maybe even why you're doing this in the first place. You just know you have to go, something has to change.

Once you take that step, though, and trust yourself, something amazing happens—you discover you can not only fly, you can soar to heights greater than you thought before you took the giant leap of faith. And the best part is that you finally tap into the power that has been with you all along. You give yourself permission to use the wings that have always been with you. Wings that were developed during the struggle of freeing yourself from the self-constructed cocoon you placed yourself in.

This transformation from the known to the unknown begins like a small snowball rolling downhill. At first, it might just be one moment of trusting yourself. One decision where you choose your inner wisdom over external expectations. It continues when you learn to say no to the life you are "supposed" to want. It keeps rolling when you stop *should*ing yourself and instead listen to what is right for you in the moment. Your awakening to your power to create an aligned life is a series of steps, one after another, helping you trust your intuition, yourself, and your ability to take the reins of your life.

Each time you honor your inner knowing and surprise yourself with your own strength, the snowball grows. One act of trust in yourself leads to another, and another, until you find yourself making choices you never thought you'd be brave enough to make. Eventually, you become someone fully living in their power and trusting themselves above anyone else in their lives.

I watched this unfold in my own life in ways that still astonish me. The woman who once believed she needed credentials to prove her value discovered she could affect millions of lives simply by sharing her authentic journey. The person who once planned everything became comfortable with not knowing what tomorrow would bring. I learned to trust that my logical mind doesn't always need the answers. I could lead myself forward on my path without knowing where that path would ever lead.

What's really fascinating is that as you begin to trust yourself more, life begins to trust you with bigger challenges and greater opportunities. It's as if the Universe says, "Oh, you're ready to play at this level? Let's see what else you can do." And instead of feeling overwhelmed by these challenges, you find yourself thinking, "Bring it on." Not because you know how to handle everything, but because you've discovered something far more amazing—you can always trust yourself to figure it out.

This is when your life begins to radically change from you shifting your belief in yourself. When you stop looking for permission from the outside world and start giving it to yourself. When you realize that your power isn't something you need to earn or prove, it's something you simply need to remember. You change not just how you see yourself, but how you react to everything in your life.

I've watched transformations like this occur in so many people in the Spirit Daughter community. They start with one small act of trusting themselves. Maybe it's finally setting a boundary, or pursuing a long-ignored passion, or speaking their truth in a difficult situation. Then suddenly, they're making bigger changes. Starting businesses. Ending toxic relationships. Moving across the country. Creating art. Not because they've become different people, but because they've finally given themselves permission to be who they really are. They finally realized their amazingness and understand that they had the power all along to manifest their life in any direction.

Take Jen, one of my yoga students years ago. She came to class every day for months, always setting up her mat in the back corner, making herself as small as possible. One day, during a particularly challenging pose, I watched her catch her own eye in the mirror. Something shifted as she realized she could breathe through the discomfort and grow. She felt the power of her body and breath connecting her to the infinite wisdom of her soul. Within six months, she had left her soul-crushing corporate job to open her own wellness center. "I didn't become braver," she told me later. "I just finally believed in my ability to breathe through the struggle and find my power in it."

Or consider Erica, a follower who messaged me about how reading my daily posts helped her recognize her own power. She had spent years in a toxic relationship, not trusting herself. She had given her power away to someone else and, in doing so, suppressed her voice.

After reading my inspiring messages, she started to believe in herself. She started to feel her power awakening and, with it, the awareness of her unhappiness. As she began to trust herself, she could clearly see how her current relationship was not aligned with her soul. Through her growing belief in herself, she took a leap of faith and ended her relationship, knowing she would endure some heartache. She trusted, though, that intuition and power would always save her and lead her forward. Today, she feels empowered in her life and attracts partners who support her. Her power had always been there. She just needed to remember it.

The transformations I've seen in others wasn't about them becoming someone new. They were about remembering who they've always been. Change occurs when you break through and challenge all the beliefs that have held you back. You access your real self, including your courage, strength, and resilience, by releasing the fear that keeps you from owning your power to create your life. And sometimes it only takes one choice outside of your normal comfort zone.

The real beauty is that this remembering helps other people connect with their power too. When you begin to live from your power, you give others permission to do the same. Your courage becomes contagious. Your trust becomes an inspiration to others. Your story becomes a road map for others finding their way home to themselves.

I think this is one of the benefits of social media platforms: While they can cause a lot of negative energies, they also allow us to share our stories with others, including people we would never have met otherwise. When I first started sharing pieces of my journey and the wisdom I gained along the way openly, something unexpected happened: People began telling me that my story changed their stories. That's the power of remembering your amazingness; it inspires others to do the same.

This journey of remembering isn't always a straight line upward. There will be days when you forget again. Days when the old doubts creep back in. Days when trusting yourself feels impossible. Your outdated but comfortable life will call you back in with its habits that feel like a worn, falling-apart blanket.

It's worth repeating: We cling to the familiar, and it can be challenging to detach from it. Even if we know we are making the right decision for our life's path. When changing our lives and leaving the familiar, we must stay in our power. We must believe in ourselves to create the life we desire while trusting that one day, our new life will feel just as comfortable as the one we left, except this one will feel aligned. This new life won't bring about tension and anxious anticipation of when it will fall apart. It will feel grounded, connected to our soul, and we will know it's the life we want to live.

It's important to understand, though, that there will be moments of doubt. I still catch myself slipping back into old patterns of seeking external approval of my choices or questioning my worth. Just last week, I found myself staring at a blank page, trying to write this book, and that familiar voice of "not good enough" started entering my consciousness. Now, though, I don't believe these messages. I listen and I let them go. I view them as invitations to remember who I am. To breathe deeply. To come back home to my own truth and remember my power to create anything I desire. I remember that I am worthy of love and belonging even if I never finish this book or no one ever buys it (as I often feared as I was writing the words you're reading now).

The key isn't to never forget. It's to get better at remembering. To build practices that help you maintain your connection to your own power. For me, that's my morning meditation, my yoga practice, my writing. For you, it might be different. Maybe it's connecting with nature, or creating art, or dancing in your living room. Whatever helps you feel that connection to your own amazingness—that's your pathway home.

Think of it like tending a garden. You don't plant seeds once and expect them to grow forever without your attention and care. You water them daily. You pull the weeds that threaten them. You make sure they get enough sunlight. Remembering your power requires the same kind of consistent attention. You need to take care of yourself.

As you continue to remember who you are, as you keep choosing trust over fear and your own truth over others' expectations, something magical happens. Life begins to flow in ways you couldn't have planned. Opportunities appear that you couldn't have imagined. You feel strength in moments where you thought you'd break. And your courage comes not from figuring everything out, but from trusting that you can handle whatever comes.

And now, I'm here to tell you that you can reach for your own amazingness too. Everything I've done in my life, you can do in yours, in your own unique way. Your journey won't look exactly like mine, and it shouldn't. Your power will express itself differently, your path will unfold in its own perfect way.

You can create any life not by giving your power away to someone else, but by owning it. By taking full responsibility for every choice and realizing that you are the creator of your reality. You are the magic. It's not out there to find, it's within.

In the chapters ahead, I will share stories from my own life and guide you through the practices that saved me and ultimately taught me how to claim my power. You'll discover tools for remembering your power, connecting to your own amazingness, and learning to trust your intuition. Because it all starts with what you already know, you just need to remember it.

I'll also help you see your challenges as what the great spiritual teacher Ram Dass calls "grist for the mill." Your struggle is your fuel, not your demise. But for now, I invite you to simply open yourself to the possibility that you are far more amazing than you've allowed yourself to believe.

Remember: The power you're seeking isn't somewhere out there waiting to be found. It's already within you, waiting to be remembered. Your journey starts with this simple truth. And you begin to fly the moment you choose to believe it.

Chapter Three
YOUR INTUITION IS SPEAKING

Awakening to your power is a journey. Even if you aren't completely there yet, that's okay. You're here. It takes time to evolve. Be patient with yourself through this process. We've planted the seed, and slowly, you'll start to awaken to your fantastic nature over time.

That's the thing about awakenings: They unfold. Yes, some come like shock waves, breaking whatever spell you're under. But most of them, the ones that really change you, slowly unfold over time in incremental steps that you can process and integrate.

Notice the little things that you take for granted each day and relish them, like the fact that you don't have to control your inhale and exhale. Or that you can control them if you desire to regulate your entire nervous system. Notice how you can change how you feel in your body with a song or how someone else feels with a smile.

Notice that you have all the answers you'll ever need to know tucked away in your amazing mind and heart. Notice your intuition.

One of the most powerful awakenings you'll ever experience, and one that certainly takes time, is awakening to your intuition. I consider intuitive knowledge our greatest superpower. Our intuition is always with us, whether we choose to listen to it or not, and it's always correct.

I firmly believe that when we are misaligned with our path, when we do things because of societal pressures or the thrill of short-lived success, pieces of ourselves die each day. We lose touch with the essence of who we are and our greatest dreams. We forget about what lights us up and makes us happy. We disconnect from the things that open our hearts and remind us of what we love most about life. We then lose our power. We stop creating the life our soul wants to live and instead give our power to success, money, or quick adrenaline spikes.

When we lose touch with our power and brilliance, we do things for the wrong reasons. We look outside of ourselves for validation and worry more about the number in our bank account than the fulfillment we feel in our souls. And while we may feel excited and even motivated about the prospect of climbing the societal ladder and being recognized for our successes, this disconnection from our soul leaves us unhappy, uninspired, and burnt-out. There are countless stories of people who are "successful" by all societal measures but, in reality, are unhappy. The day feels like a grind, and every smile feels like a lie.

I was one of those people. I was successful, celebrated, and on my way to "making something of myself." Everyone praised my work, my journey, and my decisions. I had it all together by every measure. But I wasn't happy. I felt like something was missing from my life, a big something. There was an ache in my soul and an emptiness within me I just couldn't fill. Yes, I was meeting every mark, but were they the marks my soul wanted me to meet?

Then, my intuition finally spoke up. At first, it felt like a distant call from another world. It would come at random moments during my day, bringing me words, images, or hits of inspiration that at first startled me. It was like someone else was inside my head, giving me glimpses of information, but nothing I could form into a vision just yet. It came in the form of lightbulb moments pulling my attention to a feeling I had suppressed, a detail of discomfort I had overlooked, or unmistakable signs in my path I could not ignore until I figured them out.

I remember the exact moment my intuition yelled so loud I couldn't ignore it. I was twenty-three. Until that moment, I always had a plan, or as they call it in academia, a track. I had carefully laid out all of the pieces of my life plan when I was seventeen. I would go to undergraduate school to study psychology, and since there's very little one can do with a bachelor's degree in psych, I would find the perfect graduate program and continue my studies.

In graduate school, I would find my research avenue and bury myself in a pile of data that would lead to a fellowship, then an assistant professorship, and eventually a full professorship. I would publish papers, write grants, and prove something. I would prove I was something. And I would prove that I was good enough.

Lost in the chaos of my teenage years, I had decided I needed validation, credentials, and someone else to tell me I was worthy of love, belonging, and praise. I would later find out this was the greatest lie I ever told myself. I was already good enough, but realizing that would be one of my most involved and challenging journeys.

My "let me show you how good I am" plan concluded with becoming a tenured professor at a top-rated research university. I would spend my days researching, and I would have students of my own, all of whom would respect my continued quest for knowledge.

This plan was perfect for many reasons. It checked off societal boxes of success, made me feel important, and made my parents proud. I was their only child, after all. It also fulfilled my lifelong mission of only wanting to read and write for the rest of my life. That part I had decided on when I was six.

My life was working out according to plan. At twenty-three, I was researching at a top university and on track for a doctoral degree. I was contributing my knowledge to a field I admired, and everyone seemed to think I was a rising star. My parents were proud, and I was even proud of myself. It was all picture-perfect, except for one small problem: I wasn't actually happy.

The realization of my unhappiness came to me slowly and then all at once. The tightly knit pieces of my grand life plan began to unravel shortly after I did the unthinkable. I took a break, a real one. I gave myself three months to do nothing, to be nothing, and to not think about my next steps. It was the summer before I was to start my doctoral program.

I had just spent the previous year studying neurogenetics in the basement of Johns Hopkins University, surrounded by lab equipment and rodents. I must admit, part of me lit up whenever I told people I worked in such a prestigious field. And now, having just been accepted to a doctoral program to continue these studies in the fall, I was supposedly laying the foundation for my life's work.

It was what I signed up for, so I wasn't complaining. I knew, though, that if I was to begin my next chapter in the fall with clear focus and motivation, I needed some fresh air and time away from the chaotic streets of Baltimore.

Even before my intuition became my number one guiding light, it always spoke to me. In the spring, before I took off for the unknown, I knew my heart was growing unhappy with my work. I felt tired at the start of each day, and nothing really excited me anymore. Everything felt like another thing I had to check off the to-do list. I felt like I was just getting through it all, and I knew I needed a different perspective or I was never going to make it through a doctoral program.

This break was the first time I had dared to stop moving in years. From the time I was fourteen, I bounced around from one job to another. I was a hustler, always moving and always looking for ways to gather extra cash so I could give myself the experiences I desired.

I worked double shifts waitressing during college, became a camp counselor because it paid well, and sold baggies of pot to my college friends because I was a born entrepreneur. I did all this while still finding time to sit in the woods with my crystals and astrology books. I was on a quest to uncover the underpinnings of human consciousness, including why we thought the way we did, why some people believed one thing while others believed another, and how the theory of energy fit into it all.

I began the journey of understanding the human mind in early adolescence. Somewhere between seventh and eighth grade, I decided that everything my parents had taught me was wrong and there had to be another way of looking at life. Maybe that's just how the hormones of puberty affected me, but somewhere around twelve years old, I felt like my mind woke up, and the questions about life were endless.

I could probably attribute some of my thirst for existential knowledge to my Catholic upbringing. Having religion be the answer to many of life's questions just didn't suit me. It only led to more questions. None of it added up in my mind. Some people find peace in religion, I found confusion.

I would ask my mother things like, "If God is everywhere, why do I have to go to church to pray?" I wanted to know more about evolution, the Universe, and why we were here in the first place. I remember my mother telling me at one point, "Aren't you a bit young to be asking all of these questions?"

I didn't think I was young, and I didn't think she or the Church had the answers. I did think my grandmother was onto something when she said, "Everything has a greater meaning; we just don't always know what it is."

When I demanded my mother take me out of Catholic school, she asked my uncle, a philosophy major, to talk to me, or rather deal with me. My uncle opened up his library to me. I began my ongoing search to find the meaning of life and the foundation of consciousness. There I found books like *Man's Search for Meaning* by Viktor Frankl, *The Tao of Pooh* by Benjamin Hoff, and the ancient Chinese divination text the *I Ching*. I read anything I could get my hands on that gave me a sense of order in the Universe. I wanted different perspectives, even if it conflicted with what I had always known. I wanted to expand my mind.

Finally, I felt like I had some answers or at least some support. Knowing that other paradigms of thought existed brought immense comfort to me, and it still does. I gaze at these books in my office from time to time to remember where I began, where Spirit Daughter began, in the now-yellowed pages that opened my eyes and brought some answers to a twelve-year-old me.

Throughout my adolescence and college, I studied consciousness through as many lenses as possible. I read countless books, each offering a different perspective. By the time I started college, I had studied psychology, astrology, yoga, and meditation. I also studied the human mind through the use of marijuana, LSD, psilocybin, ketamine, and even a sprinkle of cocaine. If it could alter my consciousness and perceptions, I was ready to try it. I figured I was my own greatest source of data on consciousness. I've always had a strong feeling that there was more to life than I could see and feel. I was determined to figure it out and even prove it. I also knew that one system didn't have all the answers. So, I would study it all.

To say I was ambitious is an understatement. Despite all the pot-smoking, I was a Type A personality. I needed to do something or at least know what I was doing next. Taking a break was a foreign concept to me. It sounded wonderful, though, even exotic. So, I packed up my research notes, closed the door to my Baltimore apartment one last time, and said goodbye to that life, at least temporarily. I headed west to California, someplace that had always drawn me for reasons I couldn't quite explain.

The plan was simple: Spend the summer there, clear my head, then return to the East Coast refreshed and ready to begin my doctoral program. I had no idea that a simple break would destroy the life I was building. Or rather, I had no idea that I would slow down enough to really feel and, in that feeling, discover how unhappy I was in my perfectly laid-out life.

In those long summer days, I allowed myself to feel in ways I hadn't in years. I wasn't an emotional person, per se. I rarely cried, I brushed off hurtful remarks, and I focused on my work rather than how I felt about it. One could even say I was proficient at suppressing my emotions. I had them; I just knew opening them would be like opening a Pandora's box. Who knew what I would find . . .

Feeling, though, is the root of intuition. I think that's something we don't talk about enough—intuition is a feeling. And we can only begin to hear it when we allow ourselves to feel. As I gave myself permission to feel that summer, I felt lost. I felt like I had made some mistakes. I felt like I made choices for other people and not myself.

I also began to feel the rumblings of my intuition. It started to speak to me slowly, like it knew it couldn't fully awaken until it earned my trust. So, I gave it and my feelings a chance. I began journaling each morning with my morning coffee. I practiced yoga and learned to connect fully with my breath. I let myself exhale, and in that release, I let go of some control. I unraveled a bit and relaxed enough to feel my body, my breath, and my intuition.

I didn't know it was my intuition at the time, nor would I have labeled it as such. I began by recognizing my feelings in the moment and letting them guide me to simple choices, like what I would eat for breakfast or what music I would listen to. Instead of thinking through things, I would feel my way through. I would walk into a bookstore and allow myself to be drawn to certain books, seeing them jump out at me instead of logically choosing which one I would read next.

I would open the fridge and let my body guide me to what I needed to eat instead of thinking about what I "should" eat. If I had a choice between going to the beach or staying in, I would imagine myself in both situations and then decide which one felt better. I focused on feeling, which is the best place to begin to awaken your intuition.

I made these small decisions all summer long by feeling them until the big decision of my next step was in front of me. At the end of my summer hiatus, I found myself contemplating two futures—one where I stayed on my planned path, successful but clearly misaligned, and another where I was truly alive. In the first choice, I would continue on my academic path, accomplish research goals, be praised for my efforts, and be awarded for my dedication. At the end of the day, though, I would feel empty, lost, and like I was missing something. I could feel an ache in my heart and a pit in my stomach every time I thought about returning to school and continuing on the road to a doctorate.

In the second choice, I had no idea what could happen. In the magic of the unknown, though, I could feel my limitless potential. It felt exciting, and I felt more alive every time I thought about leaving the familiar. I felt scared and nervous at the thought of leaving my academic track, but I also felt like I would be truly living my life instead of someone else's. The contrast between my two options felt dramatic. My intuition was clearly pointing to the second, uncertain, scary, yet right path. My inner voice was loud, almost annoying, uncomfortable, and could not be ignored.

My intuition woke me up in the middle of the night, nudging me out of my dreams to face my reality. I could feel what I needed to do. It was distinctly different from anxiety, which I was also familiar with. My mind wouldn't race the way it would when I was worried about something. Instead, it was quiet but for one thought: I needed to leave my doctoral program. The one I worked so hard to get into. The one my professors wrote letters of recommendation for, the one my parents were telling their friends about.

I felt pangs of guilt when I thought of all the people who had worked so hard to help me to this point. My intuition, though, and the very real feeling of knowing I had to leave it all behind, was greater than any guilt I could have ever felt. There was no denying it; my intuition had spoken, and it wasn't going to become quiet until I followed it.

Awakening to your intuition feels a bit annoying, almost inconvenient, and yet really exciting. It's like an alarm bell inside of you, letting you know you ventured off the path of your soul. It stays on until you listen. There may be a few options to snooze, but there is no off switch. Once your intuition is awake, it wants to be heard and followed. It's not always what you want to hear, but it comes exactly when you need it—right before you take a step toward a path that doesn't align with who you really are. For me, awakening to my intuition meant leaving behind a promising career in academia to follow my uncertainty. It was terrifying, but also the most liberating decision I've ever made. One that eventually led me home to myself.

Your intuition is that part of you that remembers who you really are beneath all the layers of societal expectations and self-imposed limitations. It's the voice that gives you the truth about your life when you're quiet enough to listen. Your intuition understands your amazingness. It understands your power and everything you are capable of in your life. It's connected to the part of you connected to everything in the

Universe. And it will guide you to manifesting a life aligned with your soul if you allow it.

To start awakening to your own intuition, you need to get quiet. Intuition gets lost in our noisy, busy world. This is where meditation can be beneficial, which, by the way, is challenging for everyone. More on that later, but one of the questions my community asks me the most is how to meditate correctly. If you're trying, you're doing it right.

When I first started practicing real presence with myself, my mind would race, thinking about all the things I should be doing instead. It would spin backward to the past, forward to the future, and then back around again. I would worry about what I said yesterday, an exam coming up, or if I would ever feel successful. In one minute of meditation, my mind would travel to eighteen different thoughts.

But gradually, after consistent practice, I started to hear my inner voice more clearly. It wasn't always earth-shattering revelations. Sometimes it was just a feeling that I should take a different route during my day or call a friend I hadn't spoken to in a while. But each time I listened, alignment would happen. I would feel like I was exactly where I needed to be when I needed to be there.

Following my intuition also gave me the courage to let go of any plans. Each day, I would get up and decide from moment to moment what I would do, allowing my intuition to lead me. I had relied on logic and planning for so long. Everything up to this point, I had planned years in advance. Planning was a pattern ingrained in me. It's a pattern that is ingrained in many of us. It gives us a sense of control over an uncontrollable world.

This pattern, to my surprise, was easily shifted. My intuitive mind wanted to take the lead. It had been waiting in the wings all along. Unlike my analytical mind, my intuition moved with confidence. It knew what to do and when, without needing to overthink or plan.

When I finally allowed my intuition to guide me, life began to flow. It felt aligned with everything around me, as if I had stepped into a current that had always been there. Everything started working out, not according to my "plans" but in harmony with the path I was actually meant to walk.

I firmly believe that we all have a life path, a journey our soul chooses for its energetic evolution. After all, we're all just energy, and that energy is on a continual path from one lifetime to the next. Our life path represents the journey our energy needs in this lifetime. It includes all the lessons we need to grow, all the mistakes we need to learn, and all the experiences we need to flow into the next iteration of ourselves.

That's the gift of following our intuition. When we listen to it, we align with our life path, the reason we are alive in this lifetime in this form and in this body. Once we align with this energetic path, our brain begins searching for signs and serendipity. We change the filter on our mind to let in the information our intuition is guiding us toward. When we use our intuition to program the power of our energy and mind, we can fully begin manifesting the life we were born to live.

We have many powerful tools within us designed to feel and listen to our intuition. This is how we survived for thousands of years by tuning our attention inward. Before modern devices that signal danger, like a smoke alarm, our intuition served as our warning bell. It would tell us when to run before a hyena pounced upon us. It would help us scoop up our babies before danger could even come close, and it would lead us to food through sheer gut instinct. For eons our intuition has been programming our mind to focus on what was most important for survival. It is what has guided humanity through countless generations.

You have these ancient systems within you, ready to lead you forward. You have tools built into the many layers of your energy that are ready to help you awaken to your intuition.

Your body is one of your powerful, intuitive tools. It knows things before your mind can rationalize them. Start awakening to your intuition by tuning in to your physical sensations. They're your intuition's way of guiding you toward what's right for you. This is where gut intuition comes from. Your gut intuition is also known as your survival intuition. It's connected to the millions of nerves in your stomach. This intuition causes butterflies in your belly or the feeling of being sucker punched. It speaks most loudly when you are in danger. This is the most primitive type of intuition and it's the reason you are here today: Your ancestors had a feeling in their gut that told them to fight or flee.

We've all had the experience of sensing something was off. Perhaps it was at work or within a relationship. Maybe you couldn't quite put your finger on it, but you knew something wasn't quite right. Your body felt it, even when your mind couldn't find logical answers. Something encouraged you to walk away, to create distance from a situation that didn't feel safe or aligned. This feeling is your body's amazing intuition system at work. It heightens your senses and wakes you up when something doesn't add up, even before your conscious mind can explain why.

Another powerful way to connect with your intuition is to trust those random thoughts that pop into your head. You know those moments when you suddenly have an idea to go grab coffee somewhere, then you see a sign you needed or bump into a friend? That's your intuition at work. The more you acknowledge these moments when your intuition led you to something you needed, the stronger your awareness of your intuition becomes.

During my summer away from my overly ambitious life plan, I had so many random thoughts pop up, so many hits of inspiration and physical feelings. I finally found the courage to follow them. Before this time, I had always just brushed off these intuitive nudges attempting to inspire me because they didn't fit in with the life I thought I was supposed to be living. When I experienced an intuitive "aha moment," I would ignore it and place my focus back on what gave me a sense of control. Because that's the thing about your intuition: It offers no up-front guarantees. You never know what will happen before you follow it. You just need to trust it. And that's the hardest part.

When I started trusting my intuition, though, life became easier. One day, I was standing in my tomatillo garden when I suddenly thought of calling an old friend. That call led me to my first yoga teacher, who happened to be right down the road from where I was standing. This connection ended up changing my life by leading me to study yoga and become a yoga teacher, the first step on my path to starting Spirit Daughter.

These synchronicities are the Universe's way of confirming you're on the right path. Pay attention to them. They're like little clues leading you toward your greater life plan. They also only occur when you stop forcing your life and start flowing with what's in front of you, trusting your intuition.

And yes, sometimes your intuition leads you *away* from the very thing you've been working toward.

This is where courage comes in. Following your intuition often means stepping into the unknown with no guarantee. It requires you to take risks. And it's important to understand—especially in the early days of trusting yourself—the struggle to transform is only temporary. You have to know that when you take that leap of faith, doors open that you never even knew existed.

Becoming your own inner authority takes practice. It means learning to trust yourself more than outside opinions or expectations. This journey isn't always smooth. There were times when I doubted myself, when the fear of failure almost paralyzed me. But I grew stronger each time I pushed through the narrow passage from my old life into my new one and followed my intuition. Each time I followed my intuition and it proved to be right, I learned to trust myself more deeply.

To my surprise, I also learned that there are different levels of intuition.

The first level is survival intuition, as we've discussed, gut or survival instinct. The feeling that tells you when you're in danger or when something isn't right. Everyone on the planet has access to this type of intuition given to us through evolution. Logical thinking doesn't work fast enough to get you out of the grips of a saber-toothed tiger, but survival intuition does.

Survival intuition helps us know when we need to run, fight, or freeze. It tells us when we are in danger or even when someone in our life has ulterior motives. It helps us make snap decisions that come through our very will to live.

As you deepen your connection with your intuition through trusting it, you'll start to access higher levels of intuitive guidance. There's heart intuition, which guides you toward what you truly love and what inspires you. It informs our choices by bringing our attention to what feels good to our hearts. It helps us find joy and inspiration. Then it guides us to creating more of that in our lives.

Heart intuition is different from survival intuition. It's more grounded and can arrive as a sudden knowing or a slow, deepening awareness. It helps us find our joy and love for ourselves. Through this love, we can make decisions that expand us and align with our Higher Self. The Higher Self lives beyond our ego identity, the part of our minds that wants to label and define us. I also believe that the Higher Self is the part of us that is connected to the Universe at all times.

Then, there's creative intuition, which brings new ideas and inspirations. This is the intuition that artists, writers, and innovators tap into to create something new in the world. Creative intuition helps us enter a flow state where everything else around us disappears and we tap into a special magic that only we possess. This type of intuition is what takes over when you suddenly feel yourself lost in writing, drawing, or dancing. It makes you forget about time, and you feel like you're expressing a deeper part of yourself, something even beyond your conscious mind.

Creative intuition may make little logical sense and can be greatly misunderstood by others, but it resonates with our soul. It allows us to express ourselves in a way that is unique to us.

Finally, there's visionary intuition, which connects you with the bigger picture of your life's journey. This intuition can show you glimpses of your future beyond what your logical mind can conceive today. It allows you to intuit new realities and opens the doorway to greater possibilities for your life within the larger vision for everyone.

Visionary intuition can be accessed by anyone, but I find most people have discovered this intuition to be the most challenging to follow. It's what leads to great innovations, and the people who do access and follow this type of intuition change our world. Steve Jobs was following his visionary intuition when he co-founded Apple. Oprah Winfrey tapped into her visionary intuition to start her production company, Harpo, and everything that followed afterward. John Lennon, Elvis Presley, and Jimi Hendrix used their visionary and their creative intuition to change the history of music.

During my summer hiatus, I began living from and understanding my heart's intuition. I learned to love myself by slowing down and giving myself a break from the constant pressure that comes with academic life. Instead of focusing on what I would achieve next, I focused on the present moment and that became enough for me.

The more I learned to love myself, the more I heard my heart's intuition. I started to live not just from my survival intuition but from my heart.

By the end of the summer, I was fully tuned in to my heart's messages. I had shed all the attachments I had formed to the identity of my former self. I accepted that I was not going to gain a PhD in probably anything, and I would no longer be admired for my work in research. I wouldn't be at a top university, I wouldn't be proving how smart I was, and I wouldn't be perceived as having it all figured out. I would essentially release any and all attachments to my former identity and accomplishments.

It felt a bit scary to shed these attachments, but my heart felt amazing. I could feel this was the right choice for me. And although I had no idea what I was going to do next or where I would end up in five years, I knew with every fiber of my being that leaving my doctoral program was what I had to do to figure out what would make me truly happy. The not knowing was the most challenging part, but that was the part I needed to walk through to find out who I really was and what I wanted to do with my life.

As you begin to access these different levels of intuition, you'll find yourself making decisions from a place of inner wisdom rather than fear or external expectations. You'll start to see the higher meaning in everything that happens to you, even the challenges. At the deepest level, you'll feel you are on the right path.

This is the power of awakening your intuition. It gives you a sense of trust in the journey, even when you have no idea where you are headed.

Your intuition is your direct line to the Higher Self, the part of you connected to the infinite knowledge of the Universe. It's always there, always guiding you toward your highest good. All you have to do is listen. It's your personal road map, always leading you toward your most fulfilling and aligned life. Your intuition is your greatest superpower, and if you feel lost, then it's the perfect time to start using it.

So, how do you start this journey of awakening to your intuition?

It's rather simple.

Just be.

Create space in your life to do nothing, and in that space you'll find stillness. In our chaotic lives, it's easy to get caught up in the constant doing and forget about being. But it's in those moments of nothingness that you'll begin to feel your intuition.

Try setting aside a few minutes each day for stillness. You don't need the perfect meditation cushion or to be able to sit in lotus position. Just find a comfortable spot, close your eyes, and focus on your breath. As thoughts come up, let them go, just focus on each breath, one at a time.

Another powerful way to connect with your intuition is through nature. There's something about being in nature that helps us tune in to our inner guidance. I discovered this during that summer when I was deciding to leave my doctoral program. Out of the loud city and surrounded by nature, I could connect with the part of me connected to everything, including nature.

As you start to listen to your intuition more, you might find you need to make changes and some of them might be big. This can feel scary and even cause you to want to shut down your intuition. It might mean leaving a job, ending a relationship, or starting something completely new in your life.

Growth often requires stepping out of your comfort zone. Think back to the butterfly struggling to leave its old life for a new one, not knowing if the struggle will lead to its greatest flight. You must trust that your leap of faith, that your struggle, will allow you to soar to the greatest version of yourself yet.

As you start to tap into your intuition, you'll likely face resistance—both from within yourself and from others. Your logical mind might try to talk you out of following your intuition. Others might question your choices or try to convince you to stay on a path that makes them feel more at ease.

It's important to always remember that no one knows your path better than you do. Even if you don't know what you're doing with your life, you still are the best authority on how to guide yourself forward. While we all need advice from time to time, to truly create the life you want to live, you need to trust yourself.

I faced a lot of raised eyebrows when I first started talking about astrology and energy work. There were plenty of people who thought I was throwing away my education and potential. But I chose to listen to myself, and I knew that this was my path.

I always tell people that when they begin using their intuition, it's best to start with small decisions. What does your gut tell you about where to go for lunch? Which book to read next? As you practice using your intuition for small decisions that lack large consequences, you'll find it easier to trust when it comes to bigger life decisions.

I also suggest keeping an intuition journal. Write down every time you use your intuition and if it was right or wrong. Eventually, you'll gain enough evidence that your intuition knows what it's talking about and you'll begin to trust it. This trust will help you rely on your intuition more regularly.

Awakening to your intuition is a journey and a lifelong one. There will be times when you feel connected and in tune with inner wisdom, and times when you feel lost. That's okay. The key is to keep listening.

Your intuition is one of the amazing superpowers you have and get to use in this lifetime to help you make decisions. It's your connection to the wisdom of the Universe. It's also what helps program your brain and instruct it to figure out how to manifest the life your intuition knows you want.

Every vision you want to manifest begins with you listening to your intuition. It might feel scary at first, but it can lead you to a life far bigger than you can imagine. Your intuition is the key to unlocking your full potential. It's your power to create a life that's truly aligned with who you are and the reason you are here in this lifetime.

You have all the answers within you. You just need to trust them and trust yourself.

Chapter Four
FINDING MAGIC

Remember when I told you that to feel your intuition, you needed to feel all of your emotions? That wasn't just a throwaway line. It's the key to unlocking your next level of awakening. Think of your emotions as a doorway. On one side is where most of us live—in our logical minds, our plans, our carefully constructed walls. On the other side is everything we're capable of, including our intuition, our power, our connection to universal wisdom. But here's the catch: You can't prop that door halfway open. You can't peek through and grab just the good stuff. You have to walk through completely, which means feeling everything—the joy and the pain, the excitement and the grief, the love and the rage.

The thing about emotions is that you can't pick and choose. They're a package deal. You can't just decide, for instance, that you're only going to feel joy or gratitude. To feel positive emotions, including your intuition, you must also feel the not-so-positive ones, including the ones you carefully built walls to protect yourself from feeling.

Each of us has a unique avoidance or suppression pattern, something that helps us avoid the emotions we don't want to face. These patterns may take the form of addictions, overworking, oversharing, keeping ourselves busy all the time, or overindulging in just about anything from shopping to social media. We cleverly find ways to avoid the very feelings that, once confronted, will help us transform our lives.

Feeling our emotions in their entirety unlocks a door we need to walk through to ultimately take control of our lives. Beyond that door is our intuition and the knowledge that is connected with all of the knowledge of the Universe.

Pause for a moment and take that in. You are connected to all the knowledge in the Universe and all its energy. You have pieces of stardust in your body, and you come from the same material that makes the sun, the moon, and the planets.

Energy can never be destroyed; it's just transformed again and again into different forms. The energy that makes up your very body is the same energy that swirled around a massive sun to form the Earth 4.6 billion years ago. It's been hydrogen, carbon, and helium. It's created fire, earth, water, and air. And it's taken the form of dinosaurs, trees, mountains, and you. You are connected to all of it through your intuition.

Your intuition is connected to the past, present, and future all at the same time. It exists out of the realm of time and space, meaning it's not limited by any dimension. In spirituality, there is a concept called the Akashic Field that provides a beautiful framework for understanding the limitless nature of your energy.

I first encountered theories of this field while perusing bookstores in Northern California during my break from graduate school. The Akashic Field is the spiritual theory of everything. While unifying theories of physics focus on physical matter like atoms and particles, the Akashic Field goes one step further and presents the idea that the Universe is composed of a grand field of energy, a matrix if you will, that connects everything in the Universe, including all matter, energy, and, yes, you and me.

Within the Akashic Field are records of the complete history and future of the Universe. It contains a vast library of knowledge of every transformation and journey of matter and consciousness. This includes whether it was a piece of dust that formed a supernova or the foundation of the carbon molecule that went on to form the body you are resting in right now. It includes a complete and complex dataset for every string of energy in the Universe and every pathway that energy traveled. It holds all of these things within its field, and it holds the records. It's a container and a library all at once.

The Akashic Field also holds the record of your soul. It carries a running log of every expression of the energy that composes your body, mind, and spirit. It is directly connected to your consciousness because you are always conscious of it, whether you realize it or not. And guess what? Your intuition is connected to this field, and you can access its knowledge bank at any time. I told you that you are amazing!

I discovered the reality of this field during one of my darkest moments, when traditional logic and planning failed me. The Akashic Field became my lifeline, not just an interesting concept. When I couldn't ask anyone for advice or find answers in any book, I learned to tap into this universal knowledge.

During those early days right after I left my doctorate program, when I was crying on my floor wondering what I was going to do with my life, I started noticing strange coincidences. I'd open books to the exact page I needed to read. People would call right when I was thinking of them. These weren't random events. They were manifestations of my connection to this universal field of knowledge. The more I allowed myself to feel, the stronger these connections became.

You might be experiencing these connections already without realizing it. Maybe you had a strong urge to take a different route to work and later learned you avoided an accident. Or perhaps you opened up Instagram and the exact quote you needed in the moment popped up on your feed. These aren't coincidences. They're your natural connection to the Akashic Field at work.

You are connected to the grand matrix that holds the records to the entire history and future of the Universe. You can even access these records at any time through meditation and intention. They are like a Google search for your soul. You can ask these records questions about the meaning of your life, and you can understand past lives and why you hold certain patterns. You can even get a glimpse of your future if you're open to it.

You can access all the records of the Universe, but the records of your individual soul are the ones most readily available. In order to download their wisdom and direction, all you have to do is sit with yourself and feel. You knew there was a catch, right? The secrets of the Universe and your soul's path are at your fingertips *if* you allow yourself to feel, and I mean really feel, including all the emotions that you've suppressed or avoided for years.

This one requirement of feeling explains why more people don't access this wealth of universal knowledge; feeling is challenging, not to mention uncomfortable. Most of us would do just about anything to not feel the emotions we need to. The work we need to do the most is always in the emotions we avoid. And there are so many more enjoyable things to do than sit with our feelings.

Everything from the latest app on your phone, to the TV show you have to watch, to the link for those must-have shoes that just landed in your inbox all have the same thing in common. They allow you to avoid your feelings and instead give yourself a quick hit of dopamine to make you feel good. Dopamine is a neurotransmitter in your brain that produces good feelings as a reward for certain behaviors. Tons of things elicit dopamine production, and while not all of them are negative, some common dopamine producers can be used to distract you from awakening to your pain.

I know what you're probably thinking... "Wait a minute! I thought we only awoke to good things!" Here's one of the great spiritual secrets: To awaken to all the wonderful things you are capable of, like your intuition and unlimited access to the entire record of the Universe, you also have to awaken to your pain and heal it. You need to sit with every emotion, hold it, listen to it, learn from it, and understand it. You need to understand how that pain controls you, its origin, and what it needs to heal so you can find freedom and your soul's greatest potential in this lifetime.

While "No pain, no gain" began as fitness advice, I believe it speaks to something deeper. You can't access the limitless potential of your soul and manifest the life you truly desire unless you hold your pain and heal it. You may be thinking at this point "I don't have pain" or "How do you know that everyone has pain?" We all have or have had some type of emotional pain. It's part of the human condition and a universal experience that bonds us all. In Buddhism, they explain that pain is a direct result of desire. Humans desire many things like love, security, wealth, to know the future, to understand why we're here, just as a small example. We have desires, and those desires cause suffering and pain.

Emotional pain takes the form of anxiety, sadness, grief, regret, anger, and desire, among others. It can be a result of buried trauma, feeling unloved, feeling unworthy, not fitting in with society, or simply from being human. While we have the opportunity to experience many amazing things in our human form, part of the grand experience is pain. No one gets out of it. Pain should be right up there with death and taxes. If you're human, you're going to experience pain at some point in your life.

The thing about our pain is that whether we want to acknowledge its existence or not, it still controls us. Like a puppeteer from behind the walls of our subconscious mind, our pain directs our lives. And the more we are asleep to it and ignore it, the more power it has to undermine our efforts. Our pain is what keeps us afraid of growth. It's what prevents us from fully stepping into our amazingness and taking control of our lives. It sabotages us because that part of us doesn't want to get hurt again.

Our brain unconsciously guides us to avoid any situation that will cause the same pain we've experienced. Or tells us to seek out that pain again and again until we can heal it, which is why so many of us end up dating the same type of person who keeps hurting us the same way. We want to heal, but we need to realize what we are healing from in the first place, and that means we have to lean into our pain and understand it. Not a fun practice, but an essential step to ultimately creating the life you desire most.

Our pain keeps us small and prevents us from taking up the space we deserve in life. It stops us from accepting opportunities that arrive at our door because we don't feel worthy of them. Our pain makes us feel damaged and not good enough and then creates situations that feel safe. These familiar situations, known as our comfort zones, often prevent us from taking a leap of faith into the unknown, where we could fully expand into our soul's path, the one recorded in the Akashic Field.

In the days after I left my doctoral program, I became well acquainted with my pain and all of my emotions. Turns out, I had become an expert at avoiding feelings, relying on achievements, drugs, and alcohol to turn away from what was happening inside me. When I decided to leave school, I expected happiness, excitement, and possibility. I thought I would be dancing down the streets with my newfound freedom. Sure, I had no idea what I was going to do next, but I figured I'd at least feel relieved.

I was wrong. I was dead wrong. As soon as the words tumbled out of my mouth telling my professor I was leaving my program, tears followed. I couldn't even remember the last time I'd cried, so to feel these hot, wet tears on my cheeks was a surprise, especially since I was standing in the hallway of the university's psychology department. I was so emotional that my professor told me I was having an "inappropriate reaction." She was not supportive, to say the least. But surely, after I walked out the door, happiness would take over? No, wrong again. Just more tears.

I cried for about four months. I didn't know why I was crying. I had broken the floodgates, and the tears just wouldn't stop. At the time, I didn't have any tools like meditation or journaling to help me. It was like a huge weight was released from my chest, and the weight had been holding down all of my pain. Once it was gone, everything came to the surface. In those first days of the unknown, I was lost with no direction and no clues to follow.

I desperately wanted to return to the hills of California, where I had spent the summer, but that option wasn't entirely available. My summer hiatus, where I learned to trust my intuition and decided to leave my doctoral program, was spent on a pot farm tended to by my then-boyfriend, Chad. And now it was harvest season, which meant I would just get in the way. Chad was also worried about me spending time there; this was 2004, after all, and pot had a long way to go until it would be legal.

I spent most of my time in our shared apartment in Philadelphia. Why Philly? Well, that was where I was originally from, and we had decided it was a good place for me to avoid any of the drama that seemed to always follow Chad around. He wasn't just a small-time pot farmer in

Northern California; he was part of an organization involving more than fifteen people, and Baltimore, where we had met, had become a hot spot.

When criminals say "the heat is on," they are implying that the law, whether it be the police or federal agents, is catching on to their illegal antics. They feel they're about to be caught. In my time around these guys, I always thought it was an interesting use of intuition and proof that it's not just women who have a direct connection to this power. Chad and his friends "knew" when they were being followed, when their latest safe house was no longer safe, and when it was time to get another burner phone. Baltimore was intuitively deemed a hot spot by Chad and I couldn't go back to NorCal with him, so that left me crying in Philly.

I spent my time flying between our apartment in Philly and the hills of Mendocino.

In my many alone hours, I cried. I cried because I didn't know what I was doing, or what I would do. I cried because even though I knew I had made the right decision, I had no proof of it. I cried just because I couldn't stop.

I started my day with a cigarette, a pot of coffee, and a bong. It only went downhill from there. I didn't handle my newfound freedom very well. I probably should have found a job, but one of the benefits of living with a man with a bag of burner phones is I didn't have to work. Money wasn't an issue. So, I just cried, smoked, and drank coffee until I lost my mind, quite literally.

The three months after I left my graduate program went by in a whirlwind of smoke, plane rides, and marijuana fields. One morning I sat in the bedroom in Mendocino. Something felt distinctly off in my body and mind. I was seeing colors everywhere, the walls were fading away and spinning at the same time.

Was I tripping? Had Chad slipped me LSD without me knowing? That was a possibility; he seemed to always have access to every kind of drug out there. But why would he dose me? And while I didn't really think that's what happened, I still had no explanation for why I felt like I was hallucinating.

As the ground slipped away from me and I felt the matrix of the Akashic Field holding me in midair, I took off from the farm to a friend's house. I burst into her house and declared that Chad had dosed me. My friend was very comforting and believed me. This also wasn't exactly entirely out of the ordinary for this group of people. I was in Northern California with a bunch of pot growers who followed the Grateful Dead for years, went to Burning Man, and frequented ayahuasca ceremonies. They were no strangers to hallucinating.

My friend said I could stay there for the night and let whatever it was run its course. Psychedelics usually have a lifespan of twenty-four hours tops, so I would likely feel like my normal self in the morning. I spent most of the night walking around in circles, trying to figure out what was going on with me. Was I tripping? Was I losing my mind? I wandered into the bathroom and stepped on a scale. To my surprise, I weighed 88 pounds. I clock in around 130 these days, to give you some idea how underweight I was.

I stayed up all night watching shadows dance on the walls. I talked to my ancestors watching over me, I came up with a theory of why so many people in my life had blue eyes, and I felt a serene oneness with the Universe. I felt safe, held, and peaceful. I felt connected to everything past, present, and future. And I could feel the evolution of everything before me. It definitely felt like an intense acid trip.

Luckily, I had spent many nights in parking lots after Grateful Dead concerts where all the after-show antics took place, so I was no stranger to entertaining a hallucinating mind. I patiently waited for whatever was in me to wear off, but it never did. The sun rose, and I was still seeing colors where there weren't any. I also couldn't seem to think straight.

The timeline of where I was and what I was doing was blurred. How did I get here? How long had I been here?

In the morning, I tried to play it cool with my friend. I asked her to take me home so I could gather some things to leave California, probably for good. She was still under the impression that Chad had dosed me—why would I want to stay there? To be honest, I had no idea what was happening to me; if I had been dosed, it should have worn off by this point. All I knew was that I had a sudden urge to get out of California and back home to Philly. So, I told my friend I was booking the next flight back to the East Coast. She got me back to the farm and asked if I needed anything else. I thanked her and ran into the house, still out of my mind.

I probably wasn't slipped acid or anything else because no psychedelic, man- or plant-made, lasts over twenty-four hours—so why was the paint melting off the side of the house? My mind couldn't figure out this puzzle at the time, but my intuition took over and screamed at me to get out of there and head back to Philly to recenter myself. It was also clearly time to lay off the weed.

I found Chad in the greenhouse setting up new lights for all the plants inside. I didn't know what to tell him, so I just told him I had to get back to Philly, and he needed to take me to San Francisco as soon as possible. I then called the airline and bought a one-way ticket home.

The journey back to my apartment was an awakening in itself. I'll never know what happened to me, but something cracked. Maybe it was all the crying or maybe it was all the weed smoke. Maybe it was what the gurus call a kundalini awakening, which occurs when the untapped stored energy of the body from the sacrum travels up the spine to cause an elevated consciousness and a feeling of oneness with the Universe. All I know is that I've never been the same.

I was silent the three-hour drive from the farm in Mendo to the airport. Chad said he would return to the East Coast in a few days after some things were taken care of on the farm. I was fine with that; for some reason, I didn't want him to know what was going on with me. I wanted to figure it out myself, although I probably should have asked for help instead of getting on a plane out of my mind. I wasn't great at asking for help.

The airport was intense. My mind was overwhelmed by the lights, sounds, and faint conversations I could hear from the other travelers. At some point, I felt like a guide or spirit was watching over me, ensuring I got to the terminal on time. I boarded the flight and found my seat at the window. I tried to close my eyes and rest since I had been up for what felt like days. I just kept hearing whispers all around me. Not bad ones, just pieces of everyone's conversation. My mind tried to make sense of it all as if I could figure out what was going on inside of me by listening to everyone around me.

At one point, I looked out the window at the sun rising over the wing of the plane. I cried at how beautiful it was. Each color was layered perfectly against the horizon, each shining a specific hue of light and brilliance. That sunrise brought new life to me. I felt hopeful for the first time since I walked away from my doctoral program. I felt a huge relief wash over me and knew that everything was going to work out somehow.

I made my way off the plane and back home to my apartment. When I got there, there was an unhoused man sitting on my front step. It seemed like he was waiting for me. When I approached him, he told me his name was Victor and he was from the Hopi Tribe in Arizona. He had somehow found his way to Philadelphia. For some reason, I decided to talk to him and explain what was going on in my mind for what now had been forty-eight hours. I told him I had been seeing colors and hearing sounds for days. He acted like that was normal. He asked if I had eaten;

maybe I was hungry, and that was causing the strange visions. Then he told me a story about how his ancestors would walk across the desert for days without food or water. Eventually, they would connect with the Great Spirit, who would guide them on their life's path.

I was familiar with the Great Spirit. I had used Animal Medicine Cards since I was sixteen when a woman in a mystic bookshop gave them to me. I still remember her long flowing pink skirt. Each card depicts a picture of an animal that carries a specific message and medicine from the Great Spirit, an energetic force thought by Native Americans to reside within all living beings and connected to the fabric of the Universe.

Perhaps I had opened up a level of consciousness that allowed me to connect to the Great Spirit, which I also believe is another perspective of the Akashic Field. I had forgotten about these cards, but I knew they lay waiting to guide me if I could just remember where I put them last.

Victor did have a point about food, I hadn't eaten anything in a while... He also told me that when a person goes without food or water, the weight of their physical body stops holding them back, and their spirit is free to connect with the energy of the Universe. Maybe the hallucinations weren't really hallucinations; they were reality, and my mind was finally free to see them. Perhaps I had broken my filter and my brain could perceive everything it normally keeps out to maintain sanity.

I talked to him for hours on my front step. Something about his energy grounded me. It connected me with my body and breath. At one point, he even gave me a simple breathing practice that would help replenish my depleted physical body. After what felt like hours, I started to feel like myself again, and the ground solidified below me. Perhaps this man was sent here by one of the guides I felt in the airport, a messenger, to make me feel like what was happening to me was normal. I'll never know how he ended up on my path, but I am eternally grateful to him for helping bring me back to sanity. He eventually left, and I went inside, feeling more stable than before.

I lay down on my floor and pulled my knees to my chest to breathe like Victor showed me. My breath felt expansive, like I could breathe deeper than ever before. Something within me had cracked open. Maybe my new friend was right, and I had unfiltered my mind to see a richer reality. Maybe I had a mental breakdown. Maybe I just needed to lay off the pot and cigarettes. I did recognize that I wasn't about to figure out what happened to me that night, so finally after three days, I slept.

When I woke up the next morning, I felt grateful to have made it home. I felt grateful for the man on my front steps. And I was mostly grateful that my mind felt like my own again. That was also the moment I decided I would give up my morning routine of pot, cigarettes, and coffee for something more grounding.

I saw a VHS that my mom had given me out of the corner of my eye. It was titled "Morning Yoga with Rodney Yee." It felt like a sign. I popped it into the player and practiced the simple poses to connect with my body and breath for fifteen minutes. For the first time in months, I felt at home in my body. And while I still had plenty of tears in there, all of the crying opened the door for something else. I could feel my potential, my infinite connection with the Universe, and my magic. I could even feel hope for my future, that one day I would find my path—the one my soul was here to live, and it would be beautiful.

That experience shattered more than just my normal reality. It shattered my understanding of what reality even was. When you've seen your physical reality melt away and felt yourself suspended in the infinite field of universal consciousness, you can never go back to thinking small again.

The man on my steps wasn't just a random encounter either. He was evidence of how the Universe conspires to help us when we're ready to wake up. In my most vulnerable state, when my defenses were completely down and my emotions were raw and exposed, I was able to receive wisdom that my logical mind would have normally rejected.

This is what I mean when I talk about the magic that exists when we are willing to face and sit with our most vulnerable states. When we're constantly suppressing our feelings, we're also suppressing our ability to experience the extraordinary. We cut ourselves off from the very power that could transform our lives.

While I don't suggest a mental breakdown to find your connection with the Universe or your intuition, I will encourage you to make space in your life to allow any tears that want to to come up. Let them flow. Let them break your self-imposed control devices on your emotions, including the distractions, the avoidance, and the unwillingness to feel.

Notice what you initially want to do when you start to feel. Then, instead of doing, simply be. Be with your feelings and let them open the pathway to your higher knowledge. Feel your connection with the Universe and the records of your soul stored in the Akashic Field. Feel the Great Spirit of the Universe within you. Know that you are so much more than a body and mind. You are more than your emotions and thoughts. You are a container for the limitless energy of the Universe. You are full of lifetimes of knowledge, and you are connected to the matrix that holds all of it.

This is your call to unfilter your consciousness and let it reach farther than you've ever allowed it by feeling your deepest feelings. The ones you may have avoided for years.

So how do you begin this journey of emotional awakening sans a nervous breakdown? There's no one-size-fits-all approach, but there are steps that can help you create your own path to emotional freedom.

First, create a safe container for your emotions. This isn't just about finding a physical space, though that's important too. It's about creating a sense of internal safety for whatever might arise. Think of this container as your personal energetic fortress. It's a space where you feel safe exploring and expressing all of your emotions. It gives them a place to land where they don't need to spill over into your life but can be felt, seen, and processed with compassion. This container also includes the commitment to not judge yourself for your emotions. Anything you feel is valid. There is not a right or wrong way to feel. Practice observing your feelings without judging yourself for having them.

For me, this meant learning to be an observer, like the one I used to be when I was a researcher. Scientists don't judge the results, they just observe and record. Before I could process the big emotions, I had to learn to sit with the small ones without judgment. I had to learn to say to myself, "It's okay to feel this. Whatever this is, it's welcome here."

Second, start paying attention to your emotional patterns. This is where most of us get stuck because looking at our patterns means acknowledging what we've been avoiding. Notice what you do when uncomfortable feelings arise. Do you reach for your phone? Turn on the TV? Pour a glass of wine? Just observe without judgment. These patterns are clues to what you've been avoiding.

I noticed that whenever I felt uncertain about my future, which was often during those early days, I would immediately try to make plans. I would start researching graduate schools again or looking for jobs, anything to avoid sitting with the discomfort of not knowing. Recognizing this pattern was the first step to breaking it.

Third, begin with small doses of feeling. You don't have to dive into your deepest trauma right away. In fact, I strongly advise against it. Start with simple check-ins throughout your day: How am I feeling right now? Where do I feel this in my body? What am I trying not to feel? Resist the urge to analyze or fix anything. Instead, focus on building your capacity to be present with whatever arises.

A practice I developed during those early days of awakening to my inner pain was emotional check-in. Three times a day—morning, noon, and night—I would stop and notice how I was feeling. Was I anxious, unsettled, calm, or happy? No judgment, no need to change anything, just notice. Over time, I began to see patterns in my emotions and, more importantly, I began to see how temporary my feelings were. They did not need to consume me, and they always passed.

Finally, develop and commit to practices that help you understand your emotions and process them in new ways. Follow your intuitive guidance here and find what works for you. Here are some practices that have worked for me and my community:

> **MORNING JOURNALING:** As soon as you wake up in the morning, grab your journal and pen. I suggest even keeping it by your bed. Before the to-do lists or your plans for the day take over, write a stream of consciousness. Don't hold back. Write what you are feeling, any dreams you had, what you hope for the day ahead. Let your emotions pour onto the page and observe what's there.

> **BODY SCANNING:** Spend 5–10 minutes lying or sitting quietly, scanning your body from head to toe. Notice all the sensations in the body, including where your emotions might live or be stored.

> **CREATIVE EXPRESSION:** Sometimes emotions don't want to be processed or expressed through words. Paint, draw, make music, or move in ways that allow your feelings to come out. You may find you understand your emotions from a new perspective when you understand them through creativity.

Pick something that works for you to help you feel your emotions fully, so they can then open the doorway to your intuition. Allow this to be a gift to yourself, something you do each day to honor what you are feeling and to let yourself know that it is safe to feel. You don't have to do it all at once. Start with one practice that calls to you and build from there.

And most importantly, be gentle with yourself. Some days you'll feel ready to dive deep, and other days you'll need to stay where it feels safe. Both are perfectly okay.

Through awareness, you'll become someone who can hold space for all your emotions, even the challenging or negative ones. You'll trust that each feeling carries wisdom and is worthy of your attention.

I invite you to sit with your emotions, to sit with the struggle of feeling them, and to give yourself compassion as you hold them, knowing they are the doorway to your greatest power: your intuition.

Chapter Five
BE VERY, VERY STILL

Learning to sit is the simplest and hardest spiritual practice—much like awakening to your own amazingness. Both are deceptively simple in theory but profoundly challenging in practice. Just as you can't selectively choose which emotions to feel, you can't selectively choose what arises when you sit in silence. You have to be willing to meet yourself exactly as you are.

Sitting is where all the threads we've been talking about—intuition, emotion, awakening—weave together. It's the laboratory where you discover what you've been avoiding, where you need healing, and where your power can be ultimately found. It's also where you learn to trust yourself again, and where you learn to trust your intuition. Sitting is the doorway to everything you're capable of becoming. It's where you awaken to your pain, magic, and amazingness. It's where you connect with the infinite Universe and access your soul's records. Sitting is magic. And it's fucking hard.

In the days following my nervous breakdown (or kundalini awakening, if that's how you want to see it), I decided I would focus on sitting still long enough to feel. I learned about "sitting" from the many spiritual texts I read in my uncle's library years ago. It always fascinated me that so many spiritual pathways began with just sitting. The Buddha gained all of his knowledge not by reading texts, but by sitting. He essentially did "nothing" and yet accessed everything. The yogis who created the many yoga asanas practiced in studios around the world created them by sitting for extended periods of time and following the cues of their body.

I had always associated sitting with monks in the Himalayas or some other beautiful location. It's how they found peace, connected with the divine Universe, and reached a state of calmness most of us can only dream of. And while I was in the chaos of city life, I would be like the monks and sit quietly to find peace and maybe some direction. To be honest, I just wanted direction. I didn't like not having a plan. It made me feel unhinged, like my very being was about to unravel from existence at any moment.

When I originally left my doctoral program for a life of nothingness, I thought I'd be okay with it. In reality, I think it drove me insane. So, I sat and waited for answers to flood my consciousness. I waited for my intuition to tell me what to do. I had no idea what that meant at the time. I imagined it would feel like a bell ringing in my head, waking me up to a new reality where I would know exactly what to do and when. And even though I didn't have a guarantee that my intuition even existed or would speak to me, I felt confident that when it did, I would know it. I trusted I would recognize my intuition like an old friend, guiding me to my next steps.

For the next few weeks, instead of running to my cigarettes and intricate handblown glass bong first thing in the morning, I would sit and breathe. Someone once told me that when a smoker craves a cigarette, they really just want a deep breath and moment to themselves. I gave myself those moments every morning. Space just to breathe. Each day that I managed to complete this simple yet excruciating task, I felt more connected to my body. I felt I had space between me and the rest of the world.

Those first silent moments were like facing a mirror I'd been avoiding for years. Every sensation, every thought, every uncomfortable feeling I'd pushed away came rushing back. But something else happened too. In the spaces between the chaos, I started to hear my own wisdom again.

I remember one morning particularly clearly. I'd been sitting daily for about two weeks, fighting my racing thoughts and restless body, when suddenly everything got very quiet. In that silence, I felt something I hadn't experienced since I was a child. A sense of being completely okay exactly as I was. My mind stopped looking to the future wondering what to do next. My constant questioning of my choices and if they were right vanished. I dropped into a void of nothing, where I could just be. No achievements needed, no answers required. Just me, my breath, and the powerful feeling that I was enough.

This wasn't some permanent state of enlightenment. The very next day I was back to wrestling with my monkey mind. But that brief moment of clarity showed me what was possible. It gave me a reference point for what it feels like to be truly present with myself. Furthermore, it gave me a glimpse of what it is like to fully accept and love myself—and it was wonderful. It was worth a daily commitment, as challenging as it was. I was worth it.

The hardest part wasn't the sitting itself; it was showing up to sit when everything in me wanted to run. Some mornings, I'd sit down and immediately feel like my skin was crawling with anxiety. Other days, I was flooded with memories I thought I'd buried years ago. There were sessions where I spent the entire time planning elaborate futures that would never happen, and others where I relived past conversations, creating perfect responses I'd never get to say.

But slowly, something shifted. It wasn't dramatic—more like watching the sunrise, where you can't pinpoint the exact moment darkness becomes light. I started to notice spaces between my thoughts. Brief moments where I could choose whether to follow a train of thought or let it pass by. These gaps were tiny at first, but they were inspiring. They showed me that I wasn't my thoughts, that there was something deeper and steadier beneath the mental chaos.

During one particularly challenging sitting session, when my mind was spinning with worries about what to do next, I had a breakthrough. I realized I'd spent my whole life trying to control the uncontrollable. I did this through academic achievement, through perfect planning, and through trying to predict every possible outcome. But here on my cushion, just breathing, I was practicing something different. I was practicing being with uncertainty, with discomfort, with not knowing. And somehow, in accepting that I couldn't control everything, I found a different kind of stability, one that helped me feel who I truly was beyond my careful plans and desperate attempts to hold it all together.

The sitting practice began to affect how I moved through my days. When anxiety would rise about my uncertain future, I could feel it without being completely overwhelmed by it. When my mind started spinning worst-case scenarios, I could recognize them as thoughts rather than truth. The space I was finding on my cushion was becoming available in my life.

It wasn't always profound insights and breakthrough moments. Most days were just me showing up, sitting down, and trying to stay with my breath for a few minutes. But this simple act of committing to myself, day after day, was healing something deep within me. It was teaching me that I could trust myself to handle whatever came into my life—on and off the cushion.

And yes, there were days when my mind wouldn't settle, when emotions felt too intense, and when I couldn't sit still to save my life. There were so many days that I thought I was "bad" at meditating or I was doing something wrong. But I was learning about myself. I was learning that I didn't have to be instantly good at something to pursue it. I could wade through the discomfort of learning how to do something for the first time without being perfect at it.

Meditation also gave me a new perspective on my nervous system. I could step back and feel that most days, life overwhelmed me. And even though I didn't have the language for it, I began to understand that I was a highly sensitive individual. Someone who feels everything at a turned-up volume. Through stillness, I discovered what I later learned was sensory processing sensitivity (SPS), a trait found in about 20 percent of the population. I was a highly sensitive person and every time I sat with myself I could feel that sensitivity. Most days I felt like a raw nerve with everything seeming to affect me more than others.

Being highly sensitive is so much more than having intense feelings. It's a different way of processing the world and all of its stimuli. Highly sensitive people notice more, but they also process more. They feel everything on a very deep level. Their nervous systems pick up every subtle variation in their environment from faint noises to slight changes in the light. They process it and they feel it.

I began to understand why certain environments had always felt overwhelming to me. The fluorescent lights in graduate school that gave me headaches weren't just annoying. My nervous system was actually processing their subtle flickering along with constant humming. I always had the ability to feel the energy shift in a room before anyone said a word. Turns out, this wasn't just imagination. It was my heightened sensitivity to subtle changes in body language, facial expressions, even energetic vibrations that accompany most emotions.

This sensitivity touched every aspect of my life. My brain processed information and experiences more thoroughly than others seemed to. When I felt overwhelmed by intense sensory input like bright lights or loud sounds, it wasn't me being dramatic; my nervous system was simply taking in more information. Even my physical reactions to things like caffeine and medications were more intense.

This explained so much about my life. It helped me understand why I needed to retreat to my room after social gatherings. Why certain textures in clothing bothered me from the time I could remember. It also explained why I could walk into a room and immediately feel the emotional residue of an argument that had happened hours earlier.

I had always assumed everyone was like this. Discovering I was wrong gave me a new compassion for myself. Acknowledging my sensitivity taught me how to truly care for myself. I began to understand what I needed: boundaries to protect my energy, time to decompress after being in large crowds, and an environment that supported my nervous system.

The details mattered, including the sounds outside my window, the lights overhead, the people I allowed into my energetic space. Everything had an impact. Only when I honored these needs and created the right conditions could I find the calm necessary to hear my intuition clearly.

In case you're connecting the dots here, yes, research from neuroscience supports that people with SPS have less of a filter on their brain, otherwise known as the reticular activating system (RAS). This lovely network of neurons in the brain stem controls what sensory information reaches our consciousness. The current theory is that people with SPS have a more active RAS, allowing more information into their awareness. The best part about this piece of the brain? You can influence it by setting intentions and tuning your filter to what supports them. More on that later, just know it's a very cool piece of you.

Through meditation, I learned that my lack of a brain filter wasn't a weakness to overcome or something to fear. It could actually become a strength. Yes, I felt everything more intensely, yes, I might have had a breakdown from too much information entering my consciousness, but this also meant I had access to deeper levels of insight and intuition. My heightened awareness, when properly channeled, allowed me to pick up on subtle energetic shifts that others might miss. What had once felt like a part of myself I needed to fear or guard against suddenly became a gift. One I would figure out how to use one day to help others heal, grow, and find their life's path.

But this gift required care and nurturance. I needed to learn how to protect my energy without shutting down to the world around me. I could have chosen at this point to retreat to a cave in the woods, but I didn't. I learned instead how to care for myself in a new way, one that would honor my sensitivity but would also allow me to stay connected to the world.

Meditation became my daily practice of finding the balance of staying open to everything around me while maintaining healthy boundaries and my sanity. Through meditation, I learned to recognize when I was approaching sensory overload and how to take some deep breaths to reset my nervous system before reaching that point. I learned I would never remain calm all the time, but I could recognize when I lost my sense of peace. Most importantly, I could develop skills to guide me easily back to center.

The insights about my sensitivity also helped explain why I had always sought escape through substances. The cigarettes, weed, and coffee were attempts to regulate an oversensitive nervous system. Now, through meditation, I was finding healthier ways to manage my sensitivity and my ability to perceive more than my brain found comfortable. Instead of numbing myself I was learning to work with my sensitivity, to understand what it needed and to understand what I needed. I also was learning to appreciate my gifts and my uniqueness.

My journey into meditation wasn't smooth or graceful. Learning to meditate this way—without guidance, without rules, without knowing if I was doing it "right"—was a fundamental shift for me. It was the first time I could remember that I allowed myself to be a beginner, to be imperfect, to simply learn through experience. This was huge for someone who had always abandoned anything she couldn't master immediately.

Sports are a perfect example. I wasn't naturally athletic, and my hand-eye coordination was practically nonexistent. I still remember my brief stint with field hockey in high school, which ended after I almost took someone's head off with my stick. My coach kindly suggested I try track and field instead, where I wouldn't have to make contact with anything or anyone. I opted for rolling joints in the woods with my crystals instead.

But meditation was different. Even though I wasn't "good" at it (is anyone good at it at first?), something about it called to me. Maybe it was because there was nowhere else to go, nothing else to do but sit with myself. Or maybe it was because, for the first time, I was doing something not to excel at it, but simply to understand myself better.

Over the years, I've received the most questions about meditation. My answer to all of them is just to sit. There is no right or wrong way to meditate. There is no right or wrong way to sit with your emotions. Even if you are thinking the entire time, it still counts. Even if you only make it through one minute, it counts. Lying down, sitting on a cushion, inside or out. It all counts. If you're showing up for yourself, it counts.

After two decades of meditation, I can tell you that's the most important component—just show up. Show up for yourself, for your energy, for your amazingness. When you show up, your life changes. Every day you sit on your meditation cushion, you're telling yourself that you're ready. You may not know what you're ready for, but you're ready. You're ready to learn, to evolve, to download knowledge, to connect with yourself, and to be yourself.

You're ready to put down the myriad distractions and get to know yourself on the deepest level possible. And when you show up, everything you need is revealed to you. You create space between what's happening around you and your reactions. You take time to figure out the answers you need right now. The past begins to make sense as you process it in a new light.

In the silence, it's easier to feel and recognize what makes you unique. What makes your nervous system unique, your energy unique, and your mind unique. You can awaken to your gifts and recognize what only you have to offer the world. These are the seeds of finding your true purpose in life, and they can be felt in meditation.

Sitting also lets you realize where you need some help from a therapist, friend, or another source of knowledge; you realize what you need when you show up for yourself. I know I did.

Meditation helped me feel confident enough to seek out therapy. I've been seeing someone ever since. It turns out that most people who get degrees in psychology need quite a bit of it. I was definitely one of them. Along with my daily meditation practice, I began seeing a core energetics therapist. This specific type of therapy appealed to my love of energy.

At the time, I was fascinated by quantum physics. After my morning meditation sessions, I would spend hours immersed in books on string theory and parallel universes. I believed that if we were ever to truly define consciousness and study it, research would need to combine theories of psychology and physics. I still believe this and almost went back to school to study it, but I decided to leave that project for another lifetime. I do think of it often, though, when I say that we are connected to the Universe and are the Universe itself. I believe that. I believe quantum physics will prove one day that we are energetically connected to everything past, present, and future.

In my early days of meditation, I was also obsessed with the human brain, how we thought, and if, one day, we could prove the interconnectedness of our consciousness. I wondered what had happened to me when I started hallucinating like someone who took twenty hits of LSD. Perhaps I blew my RAS? Perhaps I entered another dimension of the time-space continuum? I did see a few wormholes . . . There have been many times I wished I could have recorded the inside of my mind back then to study it and contribute my journey to science. Instead, I went to therapy.

Core energetics therapy centers around the philosophies that all healing lies within, that we are each on a creative evolution of our energy, and we comprise a unified field of body, mind, and spirit—meaning our emotions affect our body and vice versa. Core energetics also focuses heavily on the stages of consciousness we journey through from before we are even conceived.

The theory emphasizes that we need to feel a positive experience with one stage of consciousness to expand into the next. We get blocked from progressing when we don't have that positive foundation. When consciousness expansion is blocked, our life force stagnates, keeping us from our highest potential and purpose.

It all sounded great to me. I wanted to understand these levels of consciousness, including what they actually meant and how to move through them. I wanted to expand into my potential and discover the journey my life force was meant to take. If therapy could teach me that, I was all in.

In reality, I spent a lot of time hitting a foam block with a baseball bat in my therapist's office. I apparently had a lot of anger, even rage, that was blocking me. My therapist told me that connecting to that energy would allow me to move forward in my life. So, I hit a foam block, maybe even punched it. It felt good; it felt like what I needed at the time.

Then came more crying. I had a therapy session every Friday, which I would not suggest as the best day for intense therapy because it ruined every weekend. For days after therapy, I would just curl up in a ball and cry. This time, though, I was starting to understand what I was crying about. And, you guessed it, it centered around my childhood.

Growing up, I had never felt worthy of my parents' love. I felt like I had to live an unattainable, perfect life to earn their praise and acceptance. I had always gotten straight A's, did what I was told, and tried to be the best at everything to win their affection. Everything went south when I hit my teenage years, and I began telling my parents to go to hell. Until then, though, I wore perfect bows in my hair, listened to everything I was told, and was never out of line. I didn't even throw a tantrum as a kid. I learned to suppress my emotions to be the "perfect" child at a very young age.

My idea of love was that it was only given to me after I had achieved something. I had to do something and be perfect at it to be loved. There was a lot to unpack here. My current predicament found me without a plan or something to achieve, which in my mind meant I was unlovable. No wonder I was crying.

So, every Friday, I went to therapy, and every morning, I sat with myself. I would have giant revelations in my therapy session as I hit giant foam blocks with blue bats. Then, my morning meditation practice would help me integrate and understand what I was learning.

I also began journaling. At first, it was about nothing and everything at the same time. I would write a constant stream of consciousness onto the paper, without journaling prompts or guidance, just free-form writing. I would be surprised sometimes at the depth of what came out, and other days, I felt like I was writing gibberish. Either way, I let it flow.

This process—therapy, crying, meditation, journaling—became my first spiritual practice. And I committed myself to the journey. I wanted to understand who I was, why I was here, and what I should do with my life. I wanted to learn about myself, and these simple practices are where I started.

The combination of a sitting practice and therapy created a powerful alchemy in my life, one that I couldn't have predicted when I first started either practice. Meditation cultivated my ability to stay present with difficult emotions, which made therapy far more effective than it might have been otherwise. When I could sit with discomfort on the meditation cushion, it became easier to sit with it in my therapist's office. And therapy, in turn, helped me understand what was coming up in meditation, giving me space and support to make sense of the pieces of myself I was discovering in the silence of my practice.

I began to see how my patterns on the meditation cushion reflected my patterns in life. My resistance to sitting mirrored my resistance to life itself. I had always struggled with being fully present with myself and my emotions. My desire to do meditation "right" was the same perfectionism that had driven me through academia, trying to prove I was good enough. The restlessness I felt, including the constant urge to get up, to check my phone, or to do anything but sit with myself, was the same restlessness that had kept me running from myself for years.

Core energetics therapy introduced me to the powerful truth that our bodies hold our entire histories. Every suppressed emotion, every unmet need, every unexpressed truth gets stored in our physical form.

That tension in your shoulders? It might be years of holding back words you were afraid to speak. That chronic stomach pain? Perhaps it's decades of swallowing your anger. That persistent headache? Maybe it's because you insist on playing small or people-pleasing.

This understanding of the interconnectedness of our bodies and minds transformed both my meditation practice and my healing journey. My sitting practice gave me the courage to feel these stored experiences and the strength to let them move through me. Through core energetics, I learned to welcome all the emotions and understand where they were stored in my body. I would sit in meditation and feel my body unraveling. Sometimes, I would even find myself unconsciously spiraling my neck or torso. I was twisting out years of tension, by welcoming every sensation.

My therapist explained that movement was the body's natural way of releasing what it had been holding, sometimes for decades. The safety of the meditation cushion, combined with the understanding I was gaining in therapy, created the perfect conditions for this unwinding. Layer by layer, breath by breath, I was allowing my system to release what it no longer needed to carry.

These early days of spiritual practice taught me something essential about healing: It happens in spirals, not straight lines. We circle back to the same themes again and again, but each time we meet them with new awareness, new strength, new capacity. What overwhelmed us last year becomes manageable this year. What once sent us running becomes something we can sit with. The pain that used to feel unbearable becomes the doorway to our own liberation.

Eventually, I found my way to my first class in Transcendental Meditation. That's the one where you chant a phrase over and over again. I began with the phrase *So Hum*. *So Hum* means "I am That." I finally had some direction for my meditation. I would sit in the morning and say *So* on each inhale and *Hum* on each exhale. I would set a timer for twenty-two minutes and repeat the mantra until I heard the bell ring. Why twenty-two minutes? My first meditation teacher told me that the brain drops into a deeper level of stillness after certain durations of time—eleven, fifteen, and twenty-two minutes. Since I was still an overachiever, I chose the longest time.

Transcendental Meditation can be done anytime in any setting and instantly connects you to your body and breathing. I've even used it to center my body while being interrogated by federal agents—more on that later.

For now, try it yourself as you read the book. As you inhale, say to yourself, *So*. Exhale, say *Hum*. There, you just meditated. And you can continue with it for as long as you like at any time and in any place.

Meditating is like putting coins in the bank. A little bit over time adds up. Consistency—yes, you need to do it almost every day—is what really matters.

As you continue to read the pages of this book, I encourage you to meditate using this simple mantra for a few minutes a day. Yes, I'm on a personal mission to get everyone in the world to meditate because I think that is the pathway to a greater society. I also believe everyone can benefit from meditating. I know I did. Give it a try. You can always give it up later.

I suggest beginning a meditation practice with five minutes, then after a month, increasing it to eleven, and then to fifteen, and eventually, to twenty-two minutes a day of repeating *So Hum*. Learning to meditate is like building a muscle. You wouldn't begin with fifty-pound weights; you'd start small with three or five pounds. Begin meditating for a few minutes, and when that feels easy or at least approachable, increase the time. Again, there's no right or wrong way to do this. And what works for you may be different than what worked for me or someone else.

Let me be real with you about what to expect when you start sitting. Your mind will wander probably about a thousand times in five minutes. You'll get fidgety. You'll remember every email you need to send and every call you need to make. You'll wonder if you're "doing it right." Your to-do list will suddenly become crystal clear. An argument you had three years ago will pop up demanding attention. And that embarrassing moment from high school? Here it comes. This is all normal and, believe it or not, part of the practice.

Creating a dedicated space and time for your practice is also important. I found early morning worked best because my analytical mind hadn't fully kicked into overdrive yet. I found a quietness in those hours that made it easier to turn inward. I'd sit in the same corner of my room, on the same cushion, at the same time each day. This consistency helped train my body and mind to recognize when it was time to settle in.

I suggest you too have a corner set up where you can sit with yourself. It doesn't need to be elaborate, just a place to hold your cushion, journal, and a few crystals if that's what you're into. Nothing is actually required to meditate. Just yourself. You can literally do it anywhere at any time. It's important, though, to take it all in. All the physical, emotional, and energetic sensations. Don't avoid or suppress any of them. And as they arise, remind yourself that you are capable of facing them all. You are ready to feel them all and in doing so, you'll find your power.

The physical sensations of sitting become anchors when your mind wants to float away into fantasy or worry. Your breath is always with you, but there are so many other physical touchpoints available, including the feeling of your sitting bones on the cushion, the weight of your hands in your lap, or the sensation of air on your skin. When your mind wanders off into planning or remembering or worrying, you can always come back to these physical sensations. They become like old friends, reliable and always present.

The emotional sensations, as challenging as they are, that arise during meditation can be powerful guides. When you sit in stillness, you might experience waves of joy that wash over you unexpectedly, bringing tears to your eyes. You may feel a deep sadness emerge from some forgotten corner of your heart, asking to be acknowledged after being pushed aside for too long. You may also experience anger that creates heat and tension in your jaw. Welcome it all. It all will teach you something about yourself, your path, and your intuition. Even fear, welcome that too.

Each of these emotional experiences is a pathway to your intuition. Each one holds a specific key to your higher wisdom. When you allow yourself to feel anger fully—not acting on it, just witnessing it in your body—you might discover its real origin. I've always found that anger is closely linked to when our boundaries are being violated. You may not consciously realize this has happened, but meditation can help you uncover the origins of your emotions.

You also can give your emotions the full attention and care they deserve. When you sit with grief without rushing to soothe it away, you honor what you've loved and lost. You may even be able to finally feel your full joy with life instead of brushing it away as something that won't last. You'll be able to experience with your full presence. While meditation brings up your negative or not so pleasant emotions, it also connects you with your positive ones, and gives you space to really feel them.

The key is meeting each emotion with curiosity instead of judgment. Notice how they move through you. Notice how they rise, peak, and eventually transform if you don't cling to or resist them. Your inner landscape is constantly changing, and a sitting practice helps you recognize that you are the constant energy that all the emotions pass through. They will pass as everything does.

There are also energetic sensations waiting to be discovered during meditation. These can be subtle at first, but with practice, you'll be able to perceive the energy of your body. You might feel a gentle buzzing or tingling in your hands or at the crown of your head. You may feel goose bumps when you hear something true for you. Some days you'll sense a heaviness or density in your energy field that needs clearing; other days you'll experience lightness because you've released something holding you down.

Pay special attention to energy centers in your body. Places like your heart, throat, or belly, where you might feel openings or constrictions related to what's happening in your life. A tightness in your throat could signal that you've swallowed your truth, while an expansive feeling in your heart might be a sign of alignment with your path.

These energetic sensations are the deeper layers of your being becoming more perceivable to your conscious mind. Your energy body often knows what you need before your thinking mind can devise a plan. By turning your attention toward these sensations rather than dismissing them, you develop an intuitive intelligence that guides you more efficiently and confidently than logic alone ever could.

Trust what you feel. Your body, emotions, and energy field hold wisdom beyond what your mind can grasp. In sitting practice, you're not just calming your thoughts, you're tuning in to your whole being. You can begin developing a relationship with all your sensations and from there understand all the different ways your intuition speaks to you.

You're also discovering new things about yourself. Insights that can lead to your purpose, your potential, your place in the world, and even to people who enhance your path. I always say that I can manifest anything when I meditate every day, because meditation leads me to my intuition and that leads me to everything else.

Another important thing to note about meditation is your path is your own. There is no perfect way to develop the skill. Some people may never be able to sit in meditation, they need movement or something else to do while steadying their mind. Or you may need to listen to guided meditations or visualizations for a while before you learn to sit with silence. You may always need guidance, and that's okay too.

One of the most important shifts in my meditation practice came when I changed how I measured my progress. Initially, I tried to evaluate each session: Was it "good"? Did I think too much? Do I feel calm now? With practice, I learned to look for progress in my daily life instead. I started noticing small changes in my reactions to things that triggered me—I became aware of my triggers in the first place. Triggers cause a huge emotional response for no apparent reason. I started pausing before reacting to something that had triggered me. I watched myself become more aware of my intuitive hits. I started to feel more connected to myself and my body even in challenging situations. And overall, I felt okay in my body. I felt connected and grounded to my very presence, no longer needing to run or escape from it.

Most importantly, I had to keep reminding myself why I was doing this. It wasn't about becoming some perfectly enlightened being who never experiences negative emotions or challenging thoughts. It wasn't about achieving some idealized state of permanent peace. It was about feeling okay in my own body and breath. It was about remembering my own amazingness and who I really am in this lifetime.

The practice of sitting still became a daily reminder that beneath all the doing, achieving, and becoming, there was someone who was already whole. Someone who didn't need to do anything to be loved or to feel good enough.

Even on days when your mind feels like a tornado and your body won't settle, the simple act of showing up for yourself will heal something deep within. It will teach you that you don't have to earn your right to exist, that you don't have to prove your worth through constant action, that sometimes the most powerful thing you can do is simply be.

Learning to sit with myself and meditate was by far the most important step in my journey toward spiritual awakening. Eventually, I would go on to study Vipassana meditation, which would become my lifelong practice, but in my early days of meditating, *So Hum* was my best friend and became the foundation of every other spiritual practice in my life that would follow.

My meditation teacher also owned a yoga studio, so I started practicing yoga regularly with her. I quickly transformed from someone who existed solely on cigarettes, coffee, and weed to someone who went to therapy, meditated, did yoga, and journaled about nothing and everything. I still had no plan for what I wanted to do with my life, but I did feel like I had a plan for the day. Sometimes, that's all that matters, just having a plan for the day.

During this time, I spent a lot of time alone. I shut myself inside my room and pored through books I had forgotten about. Since I was a teenager, I'd collected books on astrology, Reiki, Buddhism, Taoism, aromatherapy, bioenergetics, and energy medicine. I now had books on quantum physics and string theory, and on yoga and Ayurvedic medicine.

I sat and read every day. I allowed myself to explore every topic, not choosing any one "correct" theory or perspective. I considered them all to be right in some way. Every set of ideas, from astrology to string theory, revealed a piece of the puzzle of human consciousness.

As I read these books each day, I reconnected with myself. I had forgotten who I was, lost in a sea of academic research. I had lost my curiosity, my inspiration, and my incredible thirst for knowledge. Through sitting and connecting with my breath, I reawakened myself. My mind opened and I was able to take in even more of the knowledge in front of me than ever before and connect all of it.

I didn't know it then, but I was learning powerful information that would change millions of lives one day. I also didn't know that it would help me save myself when the you-know-what would eventually hit the fan in my life and I would need every tool I had ever learned and more.

Chapter Six

THE COMFORT ZONES THAT RULE OUR LIVES

As I painstakingly learned to sit with myself and face my emotions, I also spent the next three years immersed in studying everything I could about consciousness and the mysteries of the Universe. In many ways, this was me returning to my original path before academic life took over.

I had forgotten about this part of myself. The part that was always seeking new knowledge and information about consciousness and that looked past conventional wisdom to find other lenses through which to view the world. This time, though, I was approaching these studies with new awareness, guided by both my meditation practice and my growing understanding of my own patterns from the inside out.

I could fully immerse myself in reading, meditation, and writing daily with no distractions or responsibilities. Every morning, I would wake up with the sun, roll out my yoga mat, and begin my daily rituals. I could slow down and take my time with my practices, never having to rush off to meetings or classes. I had complete freedom to structure my days around my spiritual practices and studies. Some days I would spend hours lost in meditation, other days I would write until my hand cramped, and still others I would devote entirely to studying texts about consciousness and energy. I've always been grateful for this time. It was a gift, albeit one that came with its own unique price tag.

I had the privilege of fully turning my attention to whatever I wanted to study because I was completely supported by Chad. He gave me financial abundance without question or limitation. I never had to worry about rent, bills, or even how much I spent on books and workshops. But like many things in life, this freedom came with a trade-off. The same source that provided my financial security also provided a constant undercurrent of worry and fear.

As I spent hours, weeks, and months studying astrology, crystals, Reiki, yoga, and every form of meditation I could find, Chad traveled back and forth from coast to coast, sometimes surprising me with his appearance at the house. Days would pass without word from him, then weeks. The not knowing became its own practice, a constant exercise in letting go. Most of the time I wasn't sure where he even was, or when he would return, or if he would return. Each time the phone rang, I had to prepare myself for the possibility of bad news. I feared he was always one step away from landing in a holding cell. And he was almost always unreachable and out of contact. My spiritual practices were punctuated by periods of intense worry, followed by relief, followed by more worry.

I learned quickly not to ask too many questions. Chad would often remind me that the less I knew, the better. It was for my own protection, he'd say. His business, I would later learn, was one of the largest pot-dealing operations on the East Coast and parts of the West Coast. He and his friends operated on a "need to know" basis, and apparently, I didn't need to know much. Every time I pressed for details about his whereabouts or when he'd be back, he'd gently deflect, reminding me that ignorance was my best defense if things ever went wrong.

Much later, I would come to understand that his withholding of information, though frustrating at the time, was indeed a form of protection. But I would have to wait years to fully appreciate that fact. In the moment, his lifestyle was a ball of contradicting emotions. Nerve-wracking yet exciting, terrifying yet thrilling. It was also, in its own way, somewhat inspiring.

Chad loved what he did. He was proud of it. He believed in his life path more than anybody I've ever known. He considered himself a freedom fighter. He was deliberately breaking the law for something he believed to be true. He believed it was his life's purpose to make sure the good people of America got their weed. He truly believed in the medicinal properties of marijuana and its consciousness-expanding potential. He believed in it so much that he was willing to risk his life day in and day out to follow his calling. That kind of dedication was admirable. Now, decades later, I can see how his actions back then paved the way for the present-day legalization of marijuana in many states. Chad and people like him opened the conversation on this still controversial but much more widely accepted topic.

As I watched Chad follow his vision for his life, I was a bit depressed looking at my own. I had no idea of who I was, what I wanted to do, or where I would even be in five years. I was searching for direction, but I was still in the moment very, very lost. And I was living with someone with such a strong conviction about who he was and what he was meant to do in this life that he was willing to risk it all to pursue it. He never once doubted his path or once thought about doing anything else.

I, on the other hand, questioned every day what I should be doing. Should I become an acupuncturist this week, or maybe a Reiki master? Maybe I should do nothing? I even thought I might leave it all behind and go into finance or real estate or something that could make me a lot of money, because why not?

I was fairly certain that whatever I was going to do wasn't going to be for the money. It was going to be more for the pursuit of knowledge. That's what motivated me, the quest for more and more knowledge. I just didn't know how I was actually going to turn it into a career. So, I spent my days reading books while Chad spent his days hiding from the law, flying on private planes, and counting mountains of cash.

The duality of this period in my life was striking. While I sat in deep meditation seeking inner peace, my external life could implode at any moment. While I studied ancient wisdom about living in harmony with universal laws, I was benefiting from the breaking of modern ones. While I sought to quiet my mind through yoga and breathwork, the circumstances of my life were designed to keep me in a constant state of anxiety. Yet somehow, this contradiction created the perfect container for my spiritual growth. The very instability of my situation pushed me deeper into my practices. I desperately wanted to find a solid foundation within that couldn't be shaken by what was occurring around me.

Somewhere in my studies, I discovered something powerful about anxiety: It wasn't just happening to me; I was choosing it. Like a thick sweater I never took off, anxiety was always with me, weighing me down and slightly smothering me. I worried about everything. I worried about my life, I worried about Chad's life, I worried about where I was going and how soon I would get there. I worried about making the right choices. I worried I wasn't doing enough and simultaneously worried I was doing too much.

Through my sitting practice, I began to see how anxiety quieted and even made me question my intuition. Remember how I mentioned that intuition often comes as a quiet knowing, a subtle feeling? Well, anxiety is anything but subtle. It's loud, demanding, and constantly sending out worst-case scenarios. The very noise of anxiety made it nearly impossible to hear my gentle-yet-stable intuitive guidance.

As I sat in meditation day after day, I started to notice the difference between intuition and anxious thoughts. Intuition came with a sense of calm clarity, even when the message wasn't what I wanted to hear. Anxiety, on the other hand, always carried a frantic energy, a desperate need to know, to control, to figure everything out right now. Through the practice of sitting still and observing my mind, I could finally distinguish between the two.

This was the point in my life when I truly awakened to my inner anxiety, the fears that had been with me since childhood. But more importantly, I awakened to how I was actively maintaining these fears. The constant worrying wouldn't go away no matter how much yoga I did or meditation I sat through because, on some level, I was choosing it. There was always an uneasiness, like I was holding my breath, waiting for the other shoe to drop, waiting for my entire life to crumble before my eyes. And in my particular situation with Chad, these weren't irrational fears. My entire life really could crumble in front of my eyes.

That's when it hit me. I had chosen this. Somewhere in my daily practices and weekly therapy sessions, it dawned on me that I had chosen a life where a bomb could go off at any time. I had chosen a life of anxiety because I had grown up with anxiety. There was a subconscious part of myself that wanted to continue this pattern instead of changing it or healing it. Or maybe I had created this kind of life to heal the anxiety I had lived with for so long.

I had chosen a boyfriend who sold tons of marijuana and flew in private planes across the country with duffel bags of money, a situation guaranteed to keep me in a constant state of worry. I had created the perfect conditions to continue feeling like, at any moment, everything could fall apart.

The life-changing insight wasn't just recognizing this pattern; it was understanding that anxiety had become my comfort zone. Just like the meditation cushion had become a place of peace and stability, anxiety had become a familiar home for my nervous system. Even though it felt terrible, it felt known.

We humans cling to the familiar. We're neurologically and biologically wired for it, a survival mechanism from our evolutionary past. For our ancestors, the familiar meant survival. The known path, the tested food source, the recognized shelter; these kept us alive. The unknown could mean death. This ancient programming still runs deep in our nervous systems today.

When we feel a familiar emotion, even if it's negative, we do whatever we can to continue it. We perpetuate it because it's known, and anything known feels safe, stable, and predictable. Our brain treats familiarity as safety, even when that familiarity is causing us pain. It will always choose the predictable situation over the unpredictable one, because historically, predictable meant survivable.

Until we become aware of these unconscious patterns, our brains will choose the familiar situation even if it causes anxiety or suffering. Instead of choosing situations that will heal us, we choose situations that feel familiar. Because healing means we'll feel something new, and to our ancient wiring, new equals danger. Our brains haven't yet learned that sometimes the unknown is where our freedom and our healing lies.

For years, instead of healing my anxiety and becoming free of it, I chose an unsafe situation for myself that continued the pattern of anxiety day in and day out, warranting constant worrying. I wasn't a victim of my situation, but rather, I chose it. I chose it to continue the anxiety that I had felt my whole life, like a weight around me that was so comfortable. I couldn't imagine how free I would feel without it.

I integrated this understanding into my life through my meditation practice. Instead of trying to get rid of anxiety, I began to observe how it functioned as a safety mechanism. I could feel how my body actually relaxed into anxiety because it was so familiar. I could see how my mind used worry as a way to feel in control and how anxiety gave me the illusion that I was prepared for the worst-case scenario. Through silent observation, I began to understand that my anxiety wasn't just a response to my circumstances, but rather a chosen strategy for dealing with uncertainty, one I had learned very early in life.

Where did this weight of anxiety come from? How long had it been with me, and why was I choosing situations that nurtured it? That took me no fewer than five years of therapy to figure out. The answers lay in my childhood, in patterns so familiar I hadn't even recognized them as patterns until I gave myself the space to see them clearly.

Throughout my childhood, I lived with a mother who became easily emotionally dysregulated. At any moment, she would become flooded with emotions, unable to handle them. She, like me, was highly sensitive. She did not have the tools to handle her sensitivity to the world, so she would have emotional outbursts that came in the form of yelling at my father, throwing vases across the room, and threatening to leave whenever things felt too intense for her. She was doing the best she could, like all parents. Her inability to regulate her emotions, though, created anxiety within me.

When I was growing up, before I ever met Chad, I had always felt that at any moment a bomb could go off. As a small child, I learned to become hypervigilant, always watching, always waiting, always trying to predict when the next emotional storm would hit. I developed an exquisite sensitivity to the slightest change in my mom's emotions, not as a form of intuition but as a survival mechanism.

This early training in emotional hypervigilance had two powerful effects. First, it taught me to distrust my environment. I grew up feeling that at any moment, peace could shatter into chaos. Second, and perhaps more damaging, it taught me to distrust myself. When you grow up not expressing your true emotions, your emotional reality never gets validated. You learn to question your own perceptions. Was what I was feeling real? Was I overreacting? Was I too sensitive?

The reality is that this hypervigilance actually masked my true intuition. I became so focused on scanning for threats, so adapted to living in a state of high alert, that I couldn't hear the quieter voice of my inner knowing. It's like I had the volume turned up so high on the anxiety channel that I couldn't hear the intuitive one. And that was the one with all the answers.

When we are kids, our parents are our entire world, and when they don't feel safe to be around, we don't feel safe anywhere. This is both psychological and physiological. Our nervous systems develop in relationship to our early environment. If that environment is unpredictable, our nervous systems adapt by staying in a constant state of readiness. We then carry this pattern forward, unconsciously recreating situations that match this familiar energy or state of activation.

That's exactly what I did with Chad. I recreated the perfect conditions to maintain my familiar state of anxiety. Just as I had once waited for my mother's next emotional outburst, I now waited for news about Chad's next inevitable predicament. Just as I had once tried to prevent emotional explosions through hypervigilance, I now tried to manage my fear through constant worry.

The breakthrough came when I realized that these patterns, though deeply ingrained, weren't actually me. They were adaptations, strategies I had developed to cope with an unpredictable environment. Through meditation, I began to sense something beneath the nervous tension, a deeper, quieter part of myself that remained untouched by my external environment. This was my true center, the part of me that had always known there was more to life than constantly waiting for the next crisis.

Recognizing these patterns was the first step toward empowerment. It meant I could finally see how I was choosing situations that reinforced my old ways of being. I wasn't a victim of circumstances. I was actively creating circumstances that matched my comfort zone of chronic worry. This was both devastating and liberating. Devastating because I had to face how I'd limited myself, but liberating because it meant I could make different choices.

The understanding of my anxiety was one of my greatest awakenings, the simple knowing that the hypervigilance I developed as a child stayed with me and that the adult version of myself continued to nurture that anxiety by choosing situations that reinforced it. And these choices made me feel safe.

When I stayed up late worrying about the inevitable knock at the door with the news that Chad was dead or arrested or would never be seen again—what I was really doing was recreating my comfort zone, a familiar pattern I couldn't imagine who I would be without.

In 2008, at the age of twenty-eight, I broke through. I began to understand my anxiety not as a feeling I was swallowed up by, but as a conscious choice that I could control. I did not have to be disempowered by the unhealed wounds of childhood. I could make a different choice. I could feel something different each day. I could heal and be free.

Every great transformation that we make in our lives starts with one simple choice, and this choice comes from awareness. Not the superficial awareness that comes from watching a TikTok video or having someone else point out your patterns. Transformation comes from a deep awareness that arises when we really see ourselves clearly, perhaps for the first time. This is where sitting with ourselves and our emotions becomes the foundation for our evolution. It creates the space for us to witness our patterns without immediately trying to fix or change them.

Through my own journey, I discovered that awareness itself is transformative. Once you clearly see a pattern, you can't unsee it. Once you understand why you're making certain choices, those choices lose their unconscious power over you. After I recognized my pattern of choosing situations that perpetuated anxiety, I began to notice how this pattern played out on a smaller scale every day.

I would catch myself creating unnecessary pressure in my life by doing things like deliberately waiting until the last minute to leave for appointments so I could feel that familiar rush of anxiety. I noticed I would take on too many commitments, overfilling my schedule so I always had something to worry about. I would choose friends and relationships that were unstable or dramatic, so I could always fret about if they liked me or if I said something wrong. These unconscious choices maintained my familiar and safe sense of anxiety.

We spend so much of our lives attempting to make our inner child feel safe, and so often, before we are completely aware of who we are in this world, we create a life that holds space for who we've been. Some people may choose a life where they reach milestones of superficial success and where their entire life relies on external validation because that creates a scenario that matches a childhood in which they received love only when they achieved. While others may choose a life that makes them feel powerful over others because they longed to feel that power growing up. Some may not even try to create a life for themselves because they've been taught to be a victim of their circumstances, and hopelessness feels familiar.

But awareness is power. It gives us choice. Once you see your patterns, you can begin to change them. You take back the power you gave to your comfort zones. You don't need to make dramatic changes overnight. Instead, make small, conscious choices that gradually lead you in a new direction, inspired by one moment of awakening after another.

For me, awareness looked like learning to sit with the discomfort of knowing that life could change at any moment—which by the way is true for all of us even if we aren't living with a pot dealer. Anything can change at any minute, so I learned to make peace with this instead of running away from it.

When Chad was away and unreachable, instead of spinning out into worst-case scenarios, I would practice staying present with my breath. I would remind myself that I was safe and that I had no reason to believe a catastrophe was occurring. When I felt the urge to create chaos or drama in my life through friendships, I would pause and ask myself what emotion I was trying to avoid. When I noticed myself rushing to create artificial time pressure, I would deliberately slow down, even if it felt uncomfortable.

As you walk your own path of empowerment, start by noticing where you're giving your power away. Are you choosing situations that keep you small because being small feels safe? Are you avoiding success because success feels dangerous? Are you staying in relationships that mirror your childhood wounds because they feel familiar?

Remember, we cling to the familiar because we are neurologically wired to. You're not doing anything wrong when you recreate familiar situations, you're simply acting out an evolutionary pattern that kept your ancestors safe. It takes a great deal of conscious and intentional awareness to change this pattern and invite yourself to step out of whatever comfort zone is confining you to become the next version of yourself, the one where you get to shatter the limiting beliefs that keep you playing small. Because that's what most of us are doing: We're playing small, choosing experiences that make us feel disempowered, anxious, or insecure because those are the emotions we have felt for most of our lives.

Here's what I want you to try: Throughout today and every day, notice your choices. Not just the big ones, but the small ones too. How do you choose to start your day? What thoughts do you habitually entertain? What situations do you automatically avoid or gravitate toward? Don't try to change anything at first. Just notice. Notice if you're making choices for the person you are today and the person you want to become, or if you're making choices based on who you needed to be to survive your past.

Pay particular attention to your emotional comfort zones. What feelings are you most comfortable with, even if they're not pleasant? What emotions do you avoid at all costs? Challenge yourself to be open to the possibility that negative emotions like anxiety can actually make you feel safe because you're so used to feeling them day in and day out.

There is a different way. There is a life beyond the emotions you've become accustomed to. There is a life where you can decide how you want to feel each day in the present moment. You do not have to be limited by your past or your childhood or by who you were yesterday. You can choose every day the experiences you want to feel and the situations you want to create in your life. You can choose to experience new feelings, ones you've never felt your entire life. And even if they feel uncomfortable, you will have the tools, like meditation, awareness, and your breath, to navigate the discomfort of new emotions.

There comes a moment in every journey of transformation when you must look yourself in the mirror and say, "I can do this." I can't tell you how many mornings I spent staring at myself in my bathroom mirror in Philadelphia, saying those words over and over. I can do this. I can face this fear. I can choose differently. I can be more than my patterns.

And, no, it's not just positive thinking or talking yourself into something. It's recognizing your innate power to choose, to change, to grow. Remember what I said earlier about being amazing? This is where that truth becomes your lifeline. You are amazing—not because of what you've achieved or what you've overcome, but because of who you fundamentally are: a being capable of anything, including shattering the self-imposed limitations defined by your comfort zones.

You are so much stronger than you think. You've already survived all your worst days. Think about that for a moment. You've already proven your resilience, your strength, and your ability to make it to the next day. This is your invitation to do more than just survive. It's your invitation to choose how you want to thrive.

Yes, looking at your patterns is uncomfortable. Yes, choosing differently than you have in the past is scary. Yes, letting go of familiar emotions, even painful ones, feels like stepping off a cliff. You can handle the discomfort. You can navigate the fear. You can survive the uncertainty. How do I know? Because you're already handling more than you give yourself credit for.

If you can handle living with emotions that are holding you back, you can handle the temporary discomfort of change. If you can live in situations that keep you small, you can live in situations that allow you to expand. The strength you've used to survive in limiting patterns is the same strength you can use to break free from them.

These changes that shift us from our comfort zone can come in small doses, and I suggest they do at first. Small shifts are less likely to feel jarring on your nervous system and you'll be able to integrate them with more ease. I invite you to make small, conscious choices moment by moment. Maybe today it's just pausing for three breaths before reacting to a trigger. Maybe it's allowing yourself to feel good for five minutes. Maybe it's simply acknowledging that you deserve more than your comfort zone has been offering you.

I remember the first time I consciously chose not to worry when Chad was unreachable. My body felt like it was going to explode from the discomfort. Everything in me wanted to spiral into worst-case scenarios. It was what I knew, what felt "safe." Instead, I sat with the discomfort. I breathed through it. I reminded myself that I could handle not knowing. That one small choice, that one moment of choosing differently, showed me what was possible.

Start with one small choice today. Notice when you're about to fall into a familiar pattern—maybe it's worry, maybe it's self-doubt, maybe it's anger, or making yourself small. Pause. Take a breath. And say to yourself: I can do this. I can choose something new. I can handle the discomfort of change because I am stronger than I know.

I'll admit that I don't know your specific story. Only you know your whole story. But I trust that if you've gotten this far into this book, some part of you is ready for a change. And that's all it takes. Just one small part being willing to create a new reality. Something inside of you knows there's more possible in your life. Part of you is already awakening to your own power.

Trust that part. Trust the voice that says *There must be more than this*. Trust the quiet knowing that you deserve better than what you've settled for. Trust your amazing self to handle the uncertainty of change.

You're not just surviving anymore, you're choosing. You're not just existing, you're creating. You're not just repeating patterns, you're awakening to your power to change them. And yes, it's scary. Yes, it's uncomfortable. Yes, it's uncertain. And yes, you can absolutely do this.

Chapter Seven
IT'S ALL PART OF THE PROCESS

They say the calm before the storm is the most deceptive part. Life went on for years with no real road bumps, no big catastrophes. I started to feel safe, like there was nothing to worry about. I could settle in, I could exhale. Each day started to look like the one before it, filled with meditation, yoga, acupuncture, books, runs—a perfect spiritual routine. One that was about to be shattered. The Universe, I would find out, has a way of testing whether you've really learned the lessons you think you have.

I was still in therapy, going deep into my patterns of anxiety. All those hours on my meditation cushion had taught me to recognize the subtle signs in my body that preceded anxiety—the slight tightening in my chest, the almost imperceptible shortening of my breath, the way my thoughts would begin to spiral before I even realized I was worried. I was learning to read my own warning signs, like a sailor who can sense a big puff of wind coming by watching the waves in the distance.

While I was getting better at managing my anxiety, I was still living a life guaranteed to produce it. I was also still attached, like many of us, to always needing to know the outcome of whatever I was doing. If I didn't know the outcome, or at least have some predictable path forward, I would feel overwhelmed, emotionally dysregulated, restricted in body and breath.

This attachment to outcome was what had originally driven me into academia. I had thought committing to one track with every step laid out in front of me would give me certainty, would provide guarantees. I had thought creating a ten-year plan would keep me safe, would ensure I always knew what was coming next. But if there's one thing I was about to learn, it was that there are no guarantees in life. There are no predictable paths, no matter how much you try to control them. The one very true and reliable fact of the Universe is that things always change. And things can—and will—change at any moment.

One day in March 2009 that moment arrived.

It was St. Patrick's Day. A crisp, sunny afternoon in Philadelphia. The kind of early spring day that makes you believe anything is possible. And for the first time in years, I was actually making plans—real plans with a future I could see.

I walked down the cobblestone street, mentally preparing for a yoga workshop with the world-renowned yoga teacher Ana Forrest. I had completed a yoga teacher training with her the year before and was excited to see her again at one of my favorite yoga studios. I was also thinking about my flight the next day to San Francisco, my bag already packed. I was just picking up a few last-minute items. I was scheduled to meet with an admissions director at the Academy of Art University. After years of casting about, I had finally reconnected with my childhood passion for interior architecture.

Through therapy sessions, I'd remembered how, as a little girl, I would spend hours drawing floor plans and designing spaces. Now I was ready to turn my childhood hobby into a real career. Classes would start in the fall.

Six blocks from home, my phone vibrated. A voicemail notification appeared on my screen from Chad. I stopped in my tracks. In all our years together, Chad had never once left a voicemail. Not a single time. To anyone. This wasn't normal. This wasn't right.

My palms grew instantly sweaty. My heart pounded in my chest in a way I could not calm down with my breath. I knew something was wrong. This wasn't the anxiety that had been my constant companion for years. This was different. It felt steady, solid even. It didn't feel like buzzing in my head the way anxiety did. This was a deep inner knowing. Something was terribly, irreversibly wrong.

I couldn't listen to it alone. I just couldn't. So, I turned around and walked the six blocks back to my friends' house—the couple who lived next door to me and had become my family. I spent nearly every day with them. I knew I could always rely on them.

By the time I reached their door, my heart felt like it was about to jump out of my chest. My mouth was dry, and I was dizzy from walking so quickly. Every step of those six blocks, my mind had spun increasingly horrific scenarios. Was he hurt? Killed? Had something happened to his family? This was fear, not anxious thinking, fear straight from my intuition. Something within me knew without a doubt that danger was near.

When my friend opened the door, the look on my face must have said it all.

"What's wrong?" they asked, ushering me inside.

"Chad left a voicemail," I said, the words sounding strange even to my own ears. "He never leaves voicemails."

My friends exchanged glances but didn't quite grasp the significance. How could they? They just knew their friend needed support.

I stood in their kitchen, stomach knotted so tightly I thought I might be sick, and pressed play on the message. I put it on speaker so we could all hear.

What came through wasn't a message at all—not in the traditional sense. There was background noise, muffled voices. Then, with shocking clarity, the unmistakable sound of a police officer: "Sir, step out of the vehicle with your hands where I can see them."

More rustling. Chad's voice, oddly calm: "I understand, officer."

Then silence.

Chad had apparently dialed my number as he was getting pulled over, threw the phone on the floor of the car so I could hear it all. He had wanted me to know what was happening so I could protect myself. He also knew he'd need bail; the job of figuring that out would have to be mine.

Eventually the voicemail stopped. I stared at the phone in my own hand with disbelief. I almost dropped it like a hot potato. As though if I could just get the phone as far away from me as possible, it would be like the message never happened. But I couldn't change it. I couldn't change a damn thing, nor could I control it.

My worst fears confirmed, I felt my world begin to spin. I felt like all the air had been sucked out of my body. In a whirlwind of my long-awaited nightmare, I was overwhelmed with emotion. I looked at my friends, their faces pale. We all knew what this meant, although none of us had yet grasped the extent of how far this moment would reach and shatter everything.

Then something extraordinary happened. In that moment of crisis, when everything was falling apart, and I could do nothing about it, all my years of practice kicked in as survival tools. Something deep within me took over, a voice clearer than the panic, steadier than the fear. Breathe, it said. Chant, it said. One step at a time.

My friends watched in amazement as I shifted from panic to a strange kind of calm. They couldn't believe what they were hearing on that message, but I could. I had felt this coming in my energy for months, maybe even years. I had felt it that morning right before Chad left the house. I almost begged him to stay, not to go. But I just lay in bed, listening to him get ready to leave on another unknown journey. My intuition nagged me to stop him, but I brushed it off as anxiety.

Oh how I wished it was wrong. That it was merely anxiety speaking.

For the next forty-eight hours, I broke life down to its most basic elements: breath and mantra. *So Hum* became my lifeline. *So* on the inhale, *Hum* on the exhale. Those two ancient words that I'd practiced countless mornings now became the very thing keeping me sane. Sometimes spiritual practice isn't about reaching enlightenment; sometimes it's just about making it through the next breath, the next moment, the next hour.

The yoga workshop I had planned to attend that night? Canceled. The flight to San Francisco? Missed. The future I'd just begun to envision for myself? Gone in an instant. In their place were phone calls to lawyers, desperate conversations with Chad's family, and the uncertainty of not knowing what would happen next.

I remember sitting on the floor of my living room, surrounded by all the beautiful objects that had made our place feel like home, suddenly seeing them as temporary possessions that could be taken away at any moment. The beautiful painting from our trip to Mexico. The antique desk where I wrote in my journal each morning. The cushion where I meditated. All of it suddenly felt impermanent and meaningless. Physical possessions lose their brilliance in crisis. None of it mattered.

I called Chad's sister first, my voice steadier than I thought possible as I explained what little I knew. Her silence on the other end of the line told me everything about how serious this was. They had always been prepared for this moment, his family. I suspected his family had known the risks he took, even if they never spoke of them directly.

"Call our parents," she finally said. "I'll focus on finding out where they've taken him."

Then came the call I dreaded most—to Chad's parents. His father, who was an honest man and had worked for the federal government before retiring. His mother, who had always treated me like a daughter and who had taught me the real meaning of unconditional love. She loved her kids no matter what. And she was about to prove it.

"Mrs. Miller?" My voice cracked slightly. "It's Jill. I . . . There's been a situation with Chad."

Her response surprised me. No gasp of shock, no flood of questions. Just a deep, resigned sigh. "Tell me what you know," she said.

I explained about the voicemail, the sounds of arrest, the fact that we didn't yet know where he was being held. As I spoke, I could hear her moving through their house, probably to find her husband, to begin the process we all knew would follow. The lawyers. The bail. The long road ahead.

"We'll handle this," she said finally. "We'll get through this together. Just get some rest."

There was something in her voice—not disappointment or anger, but a sadness and resignation. My own fear felt small by comparison. This was her son. No matter his choices, this was her child facing consequences that would reshape his entire life.

Later that night, my phone rang with a collect call from Baltimore County Detention Center. When I heard Chad's voice, distant yet familiar, something inside me both tightened and released. He immediately assured me he was okay, his tone deliberately stronger than I knew he felt.

A strange laugh escaped me, not knowing what to say or how to say it. When I asked what happened, though I already knew his answer would be vague, he simply said "Wrong place, wrong time." Never any details with that guy, especially on a tapped phone. Heck, my phone was probably tapped at this point. Chad would be cautious, though, till the end. Some would call it paranoia, but right now his caution seemed entirely justified.

I told him I had called a lawyer recommended by a friend to represent him. I also let him know his parents would be bailing him out as soon as they could. He didn't like that, neither did I. We had plenty of money, but bail money is different. They don't want a briefcase full of cash. They want traceable money that has been subject to taxation. So if Chad wanted out of jail, he needed help. I could tell he was disappointed I had to call his parents, but he was grateful.

He also asked if I was still leaving. Of course, I wasn't. My entire life, all my plans, my trip to San Francisco, my future in interior architecture—all of it was already on hold. How could it not be? I couldn't leave now. His sister advised me differently. She told me to get on that plane and not look back. She was a different type of woman than I was at the time. I would eventually grow into that woman, the type who puts her journey and life path first, but I was eons away from that version of myself. For now, I was committed to supporting Chad through whatever he was about to endure.

After the call ended, I sat in silence for a long time, trying to absorb what was happening. This was the moment I'd feared for years. And yet, sitting there in my living room with the evening light casting shadows across the floor, I found myself thinking not about what I'd lost, but about what remained with me no matter the circumstance.

My breath was still with me. It was steady as ever. My intuition was still here and it would never leave. I also had known what was coming before I consciously registered it. I could trust my intuition, even when everything was falling apart. These things couldn't be taken away, couldn't be arrested or detained. They were mine, permanent in a way nothing else could be.

There was something else too. A deeper knowing beneath the chaos. Even as I felt my life crumbling around me, some part of me recognized this as initiation. All those books I'd read about spiritual transformation suddenly felt less theoretical. This was the fire. I needed to walk through it to become who I was meant to be. It would take me years to fully understand the higher meaning in this darkness, but even then, I knew this was part of my path. I had the tools. I had the practice. Now it was time to use them.

The days following Chad's arrest became a master class in presence. Every step I took required me to stay centered while my world spun out of control. Simple tasks felt monumental. Even deciding what to do next seemed impossible when every choice could have life-altering consequences.

Here's the thing about crisis: It reveals not just your vulnerabilities, but your hidden strengths. In those moments when you think you can't possibly handle what's happening, something deeper than your thinking mind takes over. I watched in amazement as my body remembered its training, even when my mind was reeling. My breath would naturally deepen before difficult phone calls. My shoulders would release their tension without my conscious direction. My voice would find a steady tone I didn't know I possessed.

These weren't miraculous spiritual achievements. They were the simple, practical results of practice. Just as an athlete's body remembers its training under pressure, our spiritual practice reveals itself most powerfully in moments of crisis. It's not about reaching some elevated state of consciousness; it's about finding your ground when the earth seems to be disappearing beneath your feet. It's survival, the kind that helps you remember who you are when all you want to do is forget.

The logistics consumed the next week. Working with lawyers who specialized in marijuana cases. Figuring out how to post bail with money that didn't have an easily explainable source. Attending preliminary hearings that determined if Chad could even post bail or if he would be judged a flight risk.

Through it all, I kept returning to my breath, to my mantra. I broke each day down into its component parts: wake up, tea, meditation, shower, phone calls, legal meetings, brief moments of normalcy with friends, sleep, repeat. I didn't look too far ahead. I couldn't afford to. The future, which had seemed so clear just days before, was now a giant unknown.

Just seventy-two hours after that fateful phone call, Chad's father informed me they'd managed to post bail. Chad would be released, but with strict conditions: He had to stay within a fifty-mile radius of the courthouse. This was when another reality hit me. Chad would never again return to our Philadelphia home. Instead, he would stay at his sister's house in Virginia. His freedom, like everything else in our lives now, was conditional and under surveillance.

I found myself in that strange space between what was and what would be. I knew that something had needed to change. Something had to give. I couldn't go on the way I was living forever, nor could Chad. Looking back, I could see how the Universe had been preparing me for this moment all along. I've always found that if we don't let go with grace, the Universe pushes us out of our circumstances, sometimes with a gentle nudge, sometimes with a storm. This wasn't gentle. This was a category five hurricane.

But sitting quietly in my meditation space, still repeating my trusty *So Hum*, I began to understand something deeper about transformation. It's as if our Higher Self carefully watches over our evolution, and when we cling too tightly to the familiar, it helps us detach and venture into the unknown.

Our energy is here to evolve, change, and grow as it seeks new angles of expression. I could see now how I had been resisting this natural transformation, fighting the current of my life, exhausting myself in the struggle against my own becoming. The signs had been there for months, maybe years.

In spite of all the progress I'd made in therapy and meditation, I had noticed how stuck my energy had felt lately, how easily frustrated I'd become at nothing at all. Once again, just like when I left graduate school, my life felt misaligned, as if I was missing my target by an inch or a mile. I couldn't quite align my life. This was why I'd planned to go to architecture school. I was looking for a path because the life I was living had begun to feel off. But I hadn't acted fast enough, and then something else took over. My life was about to change in a big way and in part I felt like it was because I didn't have the courage to let go, so I was being forced to.

You can always feel the next level of your life getting ready to emerge. Your new life gently presses on the old one. It nudges you in the quiet moments, in the subtle dissatisfaction with what once felt complete. It's in the way your dreams expand beyond the containers you've built for them, in the way your heart pulls you toward something you can't quite name.

Just before life changes, which it always does, your energy will feel stagnant or stuck. You become easily frustrated, sometimes at nothing at all, and you'll feel anxious for something to occur, not knowing what that is. You find yourself going through motions of a life you've outgrown even if you aren't quite ready for the next one. Your energy will feel restless, ready for a change.

Often stagnation and restlessness are signs that you're about to break through to another level of your existence. When you resist this change, or when you simply don't let go of the old patterns, your Higher Self, who is always in cahoots with the Universe, takes over and pushes you out of your comfort zone. You can either go gracefully or with a tumble, but when your energy needs change it will find a way.

The art lies in learning to read these signs as invitations to let go with grace. In these moments of misalignment, we're being called to trust the greater rhythm of our existence. To understand that sometimes letting go is not an act of surrender, but an act of saving ourselves. That sometimes the most powerful thing we can do is not hold tighter, but open our hands and trust that what's meant for us will either stay or be replaced by something that aligns more closely with our soul's evolution.

I had just been given a wake-up call—again. I would have to make decisions about my life and even Chad's life path. For the first time in our relationship, I saw Chad with complete clarity. Not the charismatic guy I'd fallen for all those years ago. Not the self-assured freedom fighter his operations had made him appear. Just a man facing the consequences of choices he'd made long before I entered his life. Choices that, in some way, had been leading to this moment all along.

I also saw myself clearly—a woman who had spent years adapting to his life, putting my own dreams on hold, living with the constant background hum of anxiety. A woman who had survived by learning to breathe through fear, to find peace amid chaos. Yes, I had relied on his financial support, and that had given me the space to explore my inner world, a privilege I don't take lightly. But I also recognized how that dependence had fed my anxiety since it could be taken away at any moment. It was also another way I had made myself feel smaller, relying on something outside of myself.

Now that all of that was disappearing, I could see I was a woman who, despite everything, had never quite lost sight of her own path, even when it diverged from his. The realization wasn't comfortable, but it was clear: Our paths would eventually separate. The cosmic storm that had just torn through our lives wasn't just dismantling his freedom, it was dismantling the relationship we had built, revealing the ways in which it had never been quite aligned with either of our highest good.

I didn't sleep that night. Instead, I sat on the floor of our guest room, surrounded by notes I jotted down from the lawyers, numbers of who to call next, and a list of movers to call to help me clear our place out. I burst into tears. Hysterical, hot tears that fell before I could hold them back. Not just for Chad and what he faced. Not just for our relationship and what it had and hadn't been. I cried for all of it—for the life I hadn't lived while waiting for the other shoe to drop, for the dreams I'd put aside, for the woman I hadn't allowed myself to become.

The tears felt cleansing, necessary. By dawn, I felt emptied out but strangely peaceful. As the first light filtered through the blinds, I knew what I needed to do. The fires I was walking through created a direct line to my power. From this place, not panic, my next steps became clear. I would decide to support Chad in the moment, but I would make a new commitment to my life, the one outside of his, and I would learn how to put myself and my journey first. It would take time, but I would do it. I would prioritize me.

We are not static beings meant to find one perfect place and remain there. We are layers of consciousness, meant to evolve and transform. When we resist this truth, the Universe doesn't abandon us to our stubbornness. Instead, it loves us enough to make staying put more uncomfortable than moving forward.

In the end, growth isn't found in perfect stability, but in learning to accept the inevitable change of life, to bow to transformation, to trust that we are always being carried forward into new versions of ourselves. We also must trust that we will always be able to navigate the next level of our life. No matter what life throws at us, we will figure it out.

What I didn't know then, but would come to understand deeply, was that this crisis wasn't just an ending. It was a doorway. On the other side of this darkness lay a version of myself I couldn't yet imagine, a path I couldn't quite see, and a purpose I didn't fully understand. But first, I had to walk through the fire. First, I had to learn what it really means to trust life when everything familiar burns away.

I have found that the only way to heal from things you once could not bear and heartbreak that was once unbearable is to find the higher meaning. To find the greater purpose in the context of your greater life plan. And while finding the higher meaning is no substitute for the grief process, it is the way out of it.

But this journey was just beginning. It would be many, many years before I could look back and see how this crisis was exactly what my soul needed at the time. I chose it, just like I chose everything else. I chose my pain, my heartbreak.

Sometimes I look back on this time and think that maybe my Higher Self hadn't wanted me to go to school for interior architecture. Perhaps I was so off-course that some energy stepped in and threw me off my path. That's how it felt for some time, and I never once looked at going to architecture school again. I felt the Universe had redirected me in a major way and I was going to listen. I would sit and breathe until another intuitive hit came to me. I would wait for a sign or signal, because at the moment all I could do was focus on the next five minutes. Just breathing through them. The future would have to wait.

Chapter Eight
THE DARK NIGHT

The next three weeks were a blur. After Chad posted bail, I had seventy-two hours to pack up the contents of my three-story townhouse in Philadelphia. Living there meant living with the constant possibility of agents showing up at the door to raid the place, an event I did not want to experience. Beyond this practical fear, I wanted to be near Chad, and he couldn't come home.

The massive job of packing all our belongings included carefully wrapping everything from expensive artwork to handblown glass marbles, not to mention my extensive collection of crystals, ranging from raw, gem-quality aquamarine to a large, raw piece of watermelon tourmaline that was so energetically powerful that someone later in my life would tell me to bury it in the desert, because no human should own a piece of its energetic caliber.

Those seventy-two hours felt both eternal and impossibly short. I moved through rooms I once loved in a state of exhausted detachment, the soundtrack of packing tape ripping from rolls playing on repeat. The house smelled different somehow, like cardboard and dust and endings. I found myself lingering over certain objects, their familiar weight in my hands suddenly feeling both meaningless and precious at the same time. My favorite crystals radiated heat against my palm as I carefully wrapped them in soft cloth, their energy somehow amplified by the chaos around me.

The sound I remember most was silence. Not actual quiet, but the peculiar absence of Chad's footsteps, his voice, his presence. Our home had always been filled with his dynamic and unpredictable energy. Now it felt hollow, like an arena after the crowds go home. The echo of my own movements in increasingly empty rooms became a meditation of its own.

I also found myself responsible for the extensive collection of watches and jewelry Chad had gathered. He strongly believed in always enjoying his money. He knew it was fleeting and could disappear just as easily as it appeared, so he chose to wear it or hang it on the walls versus store it under the mattress. I didn't know what I would do with any of it. Wear it? Hide it under big rocks?

So, there I was in the middle of everything that represented our life together without him. Chad's family had managed to bail him out of jail, but he was under house arrest as his sister's home just outside Washington, DC, because he had been ruled a flight risk. They must have assumed there was a large sum of money stashed somewhere just waiting to help him escape his impending doom.

As I sat there figuring out what should stay out of boxes, what should go with me, and what should be buried, I couldn't help but wonder if I had called this mess into our lives somehow. I was the one who was ready for a change. I was the one who knew something had to give and the life I was living did not align with me. Chad's arrest was a wake-up call and felt like a push from the Universe. An energy outside of myself but connected to me was steering the ship, and I was along for the ride.

I held Chad's favorite watch in my hand. It was an absurdly expensive timepiece he'd bought just a few months earlier. The cool touch of the metal felt significant, like a small piece of him I could carry forward. But as I sat cross-legged on the floor staring at our former life, the immensity of the situation dawned on me anew. I realized I was sorting more than possessions, I was making decisions about which parts of our life together I would bring with me and which I would let go.

Some choices were obvious. My journals that carried my streams of consciousness as I learned to unravel my inner world would come with me. So would a small citrine tower that had helped me through countless meditations. But what about the artwork we'd chosen together? The kitchen gadgets we'd used side by side? The shared mementos from trips that now felt like they'd happened to different people? Each object carried an energetic signature, a memory, a piece of the life that was now crumbling beneath my feet.

I remember sitting on the floor of our closet, surrounded by designer clothes. When I bought them, I had felt like a princess, allowed to pick out anything in the store, no budget in sight. Some of the dresses cost more than my entire wardrobe before I met Chad. The silk felt cool and smooth against my skin, but suddenly foreign, like they belonged to someone else's life. I pulled out a single soft gray sweater I'd worn during late-night meditation sessions and set it aside. The rest could go into storage. I wouldn't need Prada for whatever was coming next.

I also felt an immense sadness. We had lived a good life together. One that was filled with time for my studies, some of the best restaurants in the world, trips with no timeline. More than any experience or physical possession, Chad and I shared a real love for each other.

My heart ached for him and what he was facing. It also ached for myself and what I was about to face. I had no idea where my life would end up now. I barely knew where it was going before this circumstance. How would I possibly figure it out now?

The emotional roller coaster was perhaps the most disorienting part. One moment I'd be organizing papers, feeling almost robotic in my movements and the next I'd be sobbing over a Phish ticket stub I'd found in a drawer, remembering the many concerts we attended together and the community of people who always surrounded us. I also felt guilty for feeling somewhat relieved that something had finally happened after years of waiting. The shoe had dropped, and I didn't have to worry about it anymore. At least that's what I naively thought.

These emotions crashed into my consciousness, overwhelming me with their intensity. I remember standing in our bathroom, staring at our toothbrushes, still side by side in their holder, and feeling waves of grief for what I was losing along with strange excitement about what might become possible, and above all, deep exhaustion. My body couldn't decide whether to cry, scream, or collapse.

One particularly difficult evening, I found myself packing Chad's favorite books—a collection of Robert Anton Wilson he'd read repeatedly, the pages dog-eared and annotated in his distinctive handwriting. I traced my fingers over his notes, these pieces of his mind, and felt a surge of love so powerful it nearly knocked me over. In the very next breath came the thought: *But was any of it real?* Had I been living in a fantasy all along? Was our connection genuine or had it been built on the adrenaline and false glamour? The doubt felt like betrayal to my heart, but it demanded to be heard.

I called my meditation teacher that night, my voice breaking as I tried to explain the flood of emotions I was experiencing without explaining the details. "You don't have to choose one feeling," she reminded me gently. "You can be many things all at the same time. And they all deserve a place in your heart. The heart is big enough for all of it." Her words gave me permission to stop trying to organize my emotions into neat categories and instead let them flow through me like waves, knowing they were all temporary and none of them defined me.

As I sat with this permission to feel everything, something shifted. Something inside of me woke up. It was an energy of strength and determination. A voice that shouted I could do this, I could get through anything, and I would. It convinced me that I would figure out my life past this point. I would figure it all out and I would keep figuring it out because that's what life is about.

I'd been moving through the packing process like a ghost, disconnected from my own experience. But as I lay on our bedroom floor at 2 a.m., surrounded by half-filled boxes, I felt my power. I placed my hands on my heart, closed my eyes, and felt my breath.

With each inhale, a subtle warmth spread through my chest. With each exhale, my shoulders dropped away from my ears. And in the space between breaths, I heard my own voice—not my anxious mind, but something deeper and steadier—say: "In this moment you are okay." And I was. I was okay in that moment. Sometimes all we have are moments and they are enough to get us through.

In that moment, I saw all the seemingly disconnected parts of my journey, including my studies in psychology, my meditation practice, my yoga training, and even my childhood, pulling together into a resilient energy strong enough to carry me through this darkness.

I opened my eyes, wiped the tears from my cheeks, and felt my spine straighten. The situation hadn't changed, I still needed to pack boxes and call lawyers. And my heart was still breaking for everything that had been and everything that would never be. I realized, though, in those moments alone with my breath in my old life filled with beautiful objects, I wasn't powerless; I was a woman with resources, both internal and external. The path ahead wasn't clear, but my capacity to walk it, step by uncertain step, suddenly was.

Part of me felt guilty that my own unwillingness to let go of a life I knew wasn't for me caused Chad to be arrested. I know this sounds irrational, of course; my staying didn't cause the DEA to investigate him. His choices led to his arrest, not mine. But in the raw moment, I couldn't shake the feeling that the Universe had stepped in where I couldn't.

For years, I'd known I needed to leave but couldn't find the strength, not because I didn't love him, but because I knew this life wasn't aligned with who I was. And now here we were. Although we were still together, I knew deep down this arrest would eventually lead to our separation. A separation that I could have chosen on my own, instead of being forced. I would hold on to this guilt for years until I finally realized that we are all on our own life path. We all decide our destiny—no one else. Not the Universe, not your planetary placements, not some version of God. We decide it all.

Our lives are in our own hands. We have the power to totally screw them up and we have the power to save them. It's all up to us. And while that may feel like a huge responsibility at first, it's also the most empowering fact any of us can ever realize. I didn't cause Chad's arrest—he did. It was his life path, the one he chose, probably even before he was born. Just like I chose my life path that came together with his for this period of time, so we could work out some karma together.

As I packed, I reflected on how this was all part of the process of my life. This trauma was placed in my path for a reason, and while I had no idea why or where it would take me, I felt a seed of peace within me knowing that it was all unfolding exactly as it needed to.

As I looked around my apartment, I realized I didn't need all that stuff. Sure, I liked it, but it didn't bring me happiness or end my suffering. What did end my suffering were my practices of mindfulness, which reduced my stress and stopped the incessant anxious thoughts. If I could avoid a downward spiral of thinking, it was a good day. So, I learned how to do that. Sure, I had thoughts, and even dark ones, but as soon as I felt myself spinning off into a sea of doom, I would use my breath and my practices to return to my center.

I detached from everything partly because I couldn't envision a future. All I had was the present moment. I believe most of our suffering as humans is because we're attached to certain outcomes. We're attached to our future visions. This attachment causes unnecessary expectations and certain disappointments. It also causes us to feel restless and agitated, waiting for our future to become our present. This restlessness causes us to accumulate material goods that make us happy for a moment as we wait for a future that we can never guarantee. These things may make our life easier, but they do not bring us true happiness. They just create more attachments.

The future is never certain. I've learned this the hard way. And even though now I am known for teaching others how to write intentions and manifest their visions of the future, I know that nothing is a guarantee. Anything can happen at any time, and that's the terrifying and magical thing about life. We can set our intentions, we can envision the life we want to live, but the minute we become attached to that future, we begin to suffer. And then we begin filling our lives with things that we don't always need.

I spent a lot of time in college studying Buddhism. While I was majoring in psychology, I minored in philosophy and anthropology. The foundational principle of Buddhism is that all suffering comes from desire. Without desire, we don't have to suffer. We may have pain, we may have disappointment, but we don't have to suffer from these things.

Suffering comes from attachment and from clinging to our thoughts. It comes from thinking we need something, someone, or even a certain future to be happy.

This Buddhist principle about desire and suffering became startlingly real to me. It was no longer a philosophical theory I once studied but a lived experience. While packing, I came across a photo of Chad and me in Hawaii the previous year. In the image, we were laughing on a pristine beach, the sunset casting everything in golden light, the moment frozen in apparent perfection.

I felt a physical ache looking at it. Along with missing Chad, I missed the certainty I'd felt then. The comfortable belief that I knew what my life would be. As I sat with the photo, I could literally feel desire taking shape in my body: tightness in my chest, a hollowness in my stomach, tension creeping up my neck. I was suffering not from what had happened, but from wanting reality to be different than it was.

I struggled with the concept of desire for years, because I was a householder and therefore had stuff. I've never been a monk, so I've always had an accumulation of goods. And while they made me happy, I realized that I didn't need them to be happy. I had to say goodbye to all those things and I was okay with that. And while this detachment wasn't a choice, it taught me a powerful lesson about possessions and happiness. The key to ending suffering while having things is to know it's okay to want, for example, a new BMW. It's even okay to feel happy when you buy said BMW. What causes suffering is if you become unhappy if that car disappears from your life.

Your work is to find internal practices that cultivate peace, joy, equanimity, love, and gratitude so you can find peace even if all the things that once made you happy are suddenly not there to fill the void. You can want shiny things, but you don't need them to be happy. The same goes for the future you may be attached to. Commit to it, work toward it, but if it doesn't evolve, still find happiness. Cultivate practices and tools that help you return to the pillars of a fulfilled life. Catch yourself when you become overly attached to a certain future to the point it causes suffering and ask yourself what would help you find peace, joy, love, gratitude, and equanimity.

The movers arrived the next morning and loaded almost everything that had been my life into a truck that would then head to a storage facility, and I didn't even think about when I would see it next. I didn't think about missing anything. I didn't even feel like I needed any of it. It may have brought me happiness once, but it didn't end my suffering. At the end of the day, it was just stuff.

I spent the next four months at Chad's sister's house processing my upside-down life and awaiting his court dates. I must say we all made the best of it. Chad's family was a treasure to be around, and within the safe haven of their home I began to feel not so alone. For the first time in years, I felt supported.

I've always managed to find the right people at the right time. Even during this really trying and challenging time of my life, the Universe handed me a complete support system. Chad's siblings and I would sit and laugh at the most ridiculous things just because we needed the stress relief and we needed each other. Every day I managed to find gratitude and even some joy that we were in this together in a way. Everything was uncertain, but I found certainty in knowing that I had people to support me no matter what unfolded.

Chad's family also displayed real unconditional love. Two of his sisters and his parents lived nearby, and they never judged him for his decisions. They never shamed him for who he was or the choices he made. They just loved him, because that's what family does. I learned that through them during a time when many families would have turned their backs on Chad or me. They didn't. They showed up with rotisserie chicken, wine, and love. They were amazing. Sure, they wanted a different future for their brother and their child, but they knew that wasn't the reality and he needed them more than ever.

His family were all working, tax-paying professionals and had chosen different roads in their lives, but they didn't impose their choices on anybody or make themselves seem better because they didn't end up on the wrong side of the law. They were the epitome of unconditional love and made me feel like I belonged and was loved for just being myself. This type of love and acceptance is one of the greatest gifts anyone can ever receive.

About four months later, Chad had his first court date. As I closed my eyes the night before, I focused solely on my breath, not allowing thoughts to consume me. I would not allow myself to spiral downward or upward and would not expect the worst to happen or the best to happen. I suspended and detached from all expectations and once again focused on my breath in the present moment. It felt like the only thing that was certain. The only thing I could rely on—a constant inhale and exhale.

The breathing technique I relied on that night and countless nights since was simple yet very effective. It's called box breathing, and I've taught it to hundreds of students since. Here's exactly how I practiced it:

I sat on the edge of the bed, feet flat on the floor about hip distance apart, hands resting palms down on my thighs. This open and supported posture immediately signals to the nervous system that you're present. Palms downward is a sign of grounding, connection. An upright spine signals that you are open, not closed off by anxiety or fear of what could happen.

I began by simply noticing my natural breath without trying to change it. Where did I feel it most? That night, I felt it primarily as a cool sensation at my nostrils, a slight expansion in my rib cage, and movement in my belly. Everyone's breathing pattern is slightly different. Observe yours at first without trying to change it. Everything starts with awareness.

After about a minute of observation, I began to gently extend my exhale, making it slightly longer than my inhale. I allowed this to happen naturally, without force. I expanded my inhale to a natural count of three or four, then exhale for a count of five or six. This extended exhale activates the parasympathetic nervous system, our built-in relaxation response.

I then began to hold my breath in for a count of four, feeling the expansion of my energy and allowing my breath to circulate through my body. It's important to remember to relax while holding the breath. Our shoulders have a way of thinking they should hold too, but it's important to consciously relax all other tension in your body while holding your breath.

Then I added the last layer—the hold out. After each exhale, before beginning the next inhale, I'd rest for a moment in the stillness between breaths. This pause might last only a second or two, but energetically it creates a space where you can drop in and find calmness even when there is no breath.

As I continued this breathing, I added in conscious awareness of three specific points: the base of my spine, where I visualized roots growing down into the earth; my heart center, which I imagined as a warm light; and the crown of my head, which I sensed as open to the sky above. This three-point awareness allowed me to feel aligned and held by the Universe. Something I needed in that moment.

When thoughts inevitably arose, including images of Chad in the courtroom, worst-case scenarios and best-case fantasies, I didn't fight them. Instead, I would silently note "thinking" and return my attention to the physical sensations of breathing. Not pushing away thoughts, not following them, simply redirecting awareness back to the breath.

After about twenty minutes of this practice, I felt a distinct shift. My shoulders had dropped away from my ears. The knot in my stomach relaxed. My jaw had unclenched. My mind hadn't gone blank. Thoughts still arose but they no longer carried the same emotional charge. I could observe them rather than being consumed by them.

The next day, Chad left to meet his lawyer at the courthouse, and I went about my day trying to keep my mind present and clear. I purposefully detached from the situation, not wanting my energy to influence what happened in the courtroom. I just held space for the best thing to happen for Chad's and my life path.

I went into deep meditation in the yoga room where I practiced. I could feel my infinite connection to everyone in the Universe, including the people involved in this case. I could feel my connection to the prosecutor, the DEA agents, and even the judge. We all just exist in an interconnected field of energy, and at any point we can tap into our connection with anyone on this planet.

I'd spent a lot of time reading books on quantum physics that presented theories on how this connection materializes and is real on certain energetic planes. I believed in these vibrational connections, but until this day I had yet to actually feel them. Maybe it was the stress of the day or my intense focus on my breath that helped me feel the infinite waves of particles that connect us all, but I did feel them in that yoga room while Chad sat in a courtroom facing his future.

As I meditated, I could also feel a sense of peace coming over me. It was a calmness, and an inner knowing that everything was going to be okay. From my center, I radiated this vibration of peace outward, hoping that it would connect to the prosecutors, perhaps calming their spirits and making them a little less aggressive as they prepared to present their case.

Energetic connections are reciprocal. They run both ways. As I was sending peaceful vibrations out, they were also coming in. I'll never know where the peaceful current began that day. It could have been the prosecutors sending me calming vibrations, albeit unconsciously. Either way, at that point in our story, I knew that everything was going to be okay for me, for Chad, and for his family.

I also once again knew that no matter what happened, I would figure it out. I was strong and I believed in my ability to figure out anything. This energy had stayed with me from the morning I was packing my boxes in Philly until right now. I was going to be okay because no matter what happened, I would figure it out. I also trusted that I had some amazing people in my life who would help me and that knowing opened my heart even more.

About an hour after this meditation session, Chad called me to say the case had been dropped. I wasn't surprised. I hadn't expected it, but I wasn't surprised. I wasn't exactly happy either because I knew there was a catch. But for now, he was a free man, and for now in this moment, everything was okay. That's all we really can ask for and the only guarantee that we have in life: that in this moment everything is okay. I would find myself saying that often to myself. Try it sometime when you're facing a challenge that feels too big to overcome or an uncertain fate you have no control over. In this moment, everything is okay.

No matter what is taken from us—possessions, relationships, certainty, even freedom—we always retain the most essential tools for our survival and transformation. Your breath is always with you. Your inner power never leaves you. They are what keep you centered in any storm.

When everything else feels uncertain, your breath remains as the one constant you can trust. It's been with you since your first moment in this world and will stay with you until your last. Between those moments lies your entire life. A journey filled with challenges that may seem impossible until you face them, breathe through them, and discover just how incredibly resilient you really are.

If you find yourself facing your own dark night, know that you are far stronger than you realize. Whatever darkness you're navigating—whether it's heartbreak, loss, failure, or fear—you have everything within you that you need to find your way through. Not because the path will be easy, but because you have the capacity to take one conscious breath after another until you make it through. And you will make it through, I promise. You may have some tears to show for it, but you'll have a deep understanding of your own amazingness that can never be taken from you.

So when life feels overwhelming, return to your breath. When the future seems impossible to face, return to your breath. When you don't know how you'll possibly figure it all out, return to your breath. Place one hand on your heart and breathe. Sometimes that's all you need to let your energy, mind, and nervous system know that you will make it through to the other side.

With each inhale, you take in new possibility. With each exhale, you release what no longer serves you. In the space between breaths lies a perfect moment of stillness where you can remember who you really are beyond all circumstances. From this center, you can face anything. From this power, you can create everything. And in this moment, you are okay.

Chapter Nine
GO WHERE YOU FEEL GOOD

It took some time for this new reality to set in. What did it all mean? Chad was a free man—for now. All of our belongings were in storage. We had no commitments, no home, and no jobs. In Janis Joplin's wise words, "Freedom's just another word for nothing left to lose." And we had nothing left to lose.

At the time, the state of Maryland decided Chad's case was too big for them and so they dropped it. And just as fast as they dropped it, the federal government picked it up. So, the big guys decided they would spend their time and money investigating the case that started with Chad and would eventually lead to fifteen more people. But, for now, he was free.

A few days after the case was dropped, Chad looked at me and said he was done making decisions, and it was my turn. It would be solely up to me where we would head next. Within a second, I replied "Santa Monica." I wanted to move to California. I wanted to live by the beach and I wanted to study anatomy and Chinese medicine at the Shiatsu School of Santa Monica.

The answer came pouring from my intuition. It was steady, firm, and grounded. It felt right and when I said it, it rang true. That was where I belonged—Southern California. He said okay, let's make it happen.

I was reminded in that moment that my intuition hadn't left me. It had been guiding me all along. Even in the moments when all I could do was put one foot in front of the other, it was with me. It never failed me or abandoned me. And I could rely on it.

This is what intuitive guidance feels like. It's not the dramatic ringing bell I had once looked for but rather a quiet, steady knowing that simply feels right. When people ask me how to recognize their intuition speaking, I tell them to notice how something feels to them. Your intuition feels true to your body and will even "ring true" in your ears. I often instruct people if they are questioning an intuitive message to say it out loud. Your intuition will sound right.

For me, it manifested as an immediate clarity about Santa Monica that I couldn't logically explain. I've been asked countless times how I ended up in LA. My intuition led me here during one of the most uncertain times of my life because it was the only decision that felt certain and true. And LA is where I'll remain until my intuition guides me somewhere else.

On the eve of my thirtieth birthday, we said goodbye to Chad's family with nothing but gratitude for the journey they walked with us. We packed up our new-but-used Toyota 4Runner—the exact model the police impounded months ago—and we started the trek across the country to California. I remember the mixture of emotions as we pulled away from the driveway, the tightness in my throat from knowing I was leaving a place of safety, the flutter of excitement about what lay ahead, and the steady weight of knowing we were most likely being watched by the Feds.

As we drove through the heartland, I watched America transform outside our windows. The rolling hills gave way to the vast plains, then the sight of the ragged edges of the Rockies. I felt myself transforming too, shedding the East Coast version of myself with every mile marker. The woman I'd been in Philadelphia had made herself small to fit into Chad's world. I'd handed over my power piece by piece, letting him make every decision from where we'd eat to where we would vacation. I relied on him for emotional stability and strength, always feeling like I was the needy one in the relationship.

Now, as we drove away from our old life. I felt my breath deepen. For the first time in years, I was the one making the decisions, including where we were going to live. I was the one who felt stable, in control of my emotions, with him relying on me for strength. It was an entirely different dynamic in our relationship, and it felt like I was coming home to myself.

At the time, the Feds were already subpoenaing many people we knew and were closely investigating Chad's operation. We glanced in the rearview mirror more often than most travelers, paranoid we were being followed. We wondered if that same blue sedan had been behind us since Oklahoma City, or if the truck that pulled into the rest stop alongside us was just a coincidence.

I remember one night, somewhere in Utah, stepping out of the car at a gas station and looking up at the many stars that filled the night sky. They seemed brighter than ever and there were so many of them compared to the light-polluted skies of the East Coast. I stood there, breathing in the cold, clear air, feeling both incredibly small beneath them and somehow more connected to something larger than federal investigations and legal troubles. I was part of the Universe, and it would hold me through everything. I was also connected to all the wisdom held in those stars. They were guiding me, and I was guiding myself.

One day we were soaking up the warm sun on the beach at Lake Tahoe and Chad got a call that one of his very close acquaintances had just been subpoenaed. They were going in for questioning the next week. This freaked Chad out, and he sprang into action. He lived by the philosophy that worrying was a waste of energy. He believed it was better to save your energy for action. So, we immediately gathered our few belongings and checked out of the hotel for fear the Feds would find us next.

I had grown accustomed to my nervous system getting rattled by a phone call or an encrypted message. I was beyond letting new developments in his case bother me. I took solace in my breath and practiced detaching from any outcome. I had no idea what would happen to Chad or me, but I was pretty sure I'd be able to breathe. I focused on that, remembering not to indulge my thinking mind, which wanted to run wild with possibilities.

This kind of mindfulness is a muscle. You must practice it over and over again. You must commit to it fully and commit to not following the path of your thinking mind into a plethora of "what if" scenarios. In a stressful environment, I could choose to either indulge my anxious thoughts or try to live beyond them.

You don't need to be under federal investigation to learn to do this. Anyone can train their attention and focus. Like everything in life, it begins with awareness. It continues with the breath, and it becomes particularly powerful when you say no to the thoughts spiraling in your head.

Try this practice when your mind starts racing with worry: When you notice the thought pattern beginning, take a deep, conscious breath. Then say to yourself: "No, not this time." Cut your thoughts off at the pass, don't allow them to take hold. Stop the spiral even before it starts. Say no and let it go. Drop it and redirect your attention to something else. Return to your breath, feel your feet on the ground, study the color on the walls, just don't allow the thoughts to take over. Repeat this process as often as necessary throughout your day, creating a boundary between you and the thoughts that don't serve you.

It takes time and effort to train your mind and energy this way. Once you commit, though, it becomes your automatic response to stress. This is true freedom, your power, and what you need to rise to your greatest potential. Your thoughts are not who you are. They do not define you. You can control them and take your power back.

I continually put my thoughts in check during this time, simply by saying no. When we left the hotel in Tahoe, I put my thinking mind at ease with my breath and got in the car to journey to our final destination. On the drive, I managed to find a tiny place to sublet for one week in Venice, California, right next to Santa Monica.

I remember landing in Venice, walking down the boardwalk, the scent of ocean salt mingling with incense and coffee from the sidewalk cafes. I watched artists painting on the concrete walls, musicians playing instruments, and people from every walk of life coexisting in this beachside wonderland.

On my second day there, I found myself sitting on the concrete steps overlooking the Venice Beach skate park. For hours, I watched skateboarders of all ages carving smooth lines across the concrete bowls, their bodies in harmony with their boards. They were completely immersed in the moment—no phones, no distractions, just pure presence. A teenage boy would attempt the same trick over and over, falling repeatedly but getting up each time with the same determined focus. When he finally landed it, his face lit up with a joy so pure that I couldn't help but smile too.

I realized I was witnessing freedom in its purest form. These skateboarders weren't wealthy by conventional standards, but they possessed something far more valuable: the ability to be fully present with themselves. They were living one moment at a time. They weren't worrying about uncontrollable and uncertain futures. They were simply here, now, doing exactly what they wanted to do with complete commitment and joy.

The moment my feet later touched Abbot Kinney Boulevard something clicked inside me. Venice was the first place in my entire life where I felt like I was home.

This was where I belonged. I knew it and I had known it all along. I felt in that moment that everything that happened so far in my life had led me to this place. Its energy aligned with my soul, and I knew the very earth I was standing on would support me in becoming the person I was meant to be.

The people in Venice seemed free and, at the time, that was all I wanted. Freedom not just from the law but also from society's expectations. I didn't want anyone questioning if I was going to get married, or have kids, or grow up to have a 401(k). I just wanted to be free to be myself and find my own flow. I wanted to find the thing that I could fully immerse myself in moment to moment without thinking about anything else.

Even in this complicated, challenging circumstance, I was able to hear my intuition clearly and follow it. I knew I had landed in the right corner of the world for my life path, and I knew my life would unfold exactly as it needed to.

After one week in Venice, I found the perfect apartment on the beach one block from the school I wanted to attend. It felt like a sign I was on the right track. It was another sublet we could anonymously rent. And even though no one was actually indicted at the time, it felt safer to keep our names off of lease agreements and utility bills.

The four-block radius around that apartment became my entire world. I could walk to the Shiatsu school every day. I could walk to two yoga studios—some of the best in the country. I could walk to a café that was filled with people at 11 a.m. on a Tuesday. I could feel I was part of something bigger than myself. I can't explain it, but Los Angeles is my place. It suits my energy.

Every location on the planet holds a certain energetic frequency. Since we are energetic beings, I believe we all have a locational energetic match. It's a place where you feel alive, inspired, and you know your soul belongs there. Every time I go back to the East Coast, where I am originally from, I feel tired, sluggish, and in a lower vibration. When I get back to LA, I feel like I can breathe again. Those first weeks in LA made me believe my story was going to turn out okay. That I was going to make it through whatever hell I was walking in because, somehow, I had landed in a location that could support me. I was aligned with where I needed to be.

Location isn't talked about enough. Where you live matters to your energy. It's nearly impossible to live a fulfilled, aligned life until you find your place. Here's how to determine if a location is right for you:

Start by noticing your energy levels when you're in different places. Do you feel naturally energized in certain locations, or constantly drained? Pay close attention to synchronicities too—those moments when things just flow easily versus places where everything feels like a struggle. Your physical body offers important clues as well; notice if your body naturally relaxes somewhere or if you're constantly tense for no apparent reason.

Sometimes a place will even "call" to you through dreams, recurring thoughts, or media that keeps bringing a location to your attention. Before making any major moves, try to spend some time there to get beyond the vacation feeling and into the rhythm of daily life. Most importantly, trust yourself—the right place often just "feels right" in a way that transcends logic.

It varies for everyone, which is why it's important to find your partner's location too. The land beneath us holds energy. And we either align with that energy or we don't. Furthermore, that energy either aligns with our soul's purpose or it doesn't. When you find a location that energetically aligns with your soul's energy, everything begins to flow.

That's what I started to experience once I landed in LA. I found the perfect apartment; I met the people I needed to support me. I felt energized, inspired, and open to what I would find next on my path, whether it be a matcha smoothie or a new form of healing. It would be years until I found my true calling, but I knew I was on the path and it began in that sublet apartment on the beach.

Right away, I felt happy. It didn't matter how I'd gotten there or that the Feds could subpoena me at any moment. It didn't matter that they could take Chad away, seize my possessions, upend everything. I was grateful. Every day I walked outside and saw the Pacific Ocean, I felt at ease and expansive. I could sit at the water's edge and breathe with the waves, letting them cleanse the stress that had gathered on my soul.

I was grateful I could fill my days studying Chinese medicine with people who believed in it as deeply as I did. I was grateful that I had decided to leave research all those years ago. I was grateful for everything that had happened in my life up to this point, including Chad's arrest, having to live in Chad's sister's house for four months and for the chance to find where I belonged. I was exploding with appreciation for the choices and the freedom in front of me. I was so grateful to be exactly where I was and that gratitude saved me.

Try this practice: Each morning, stand at your window or step outside. Notice three things you can see that fill you with gratitude. Feel the appreciation in your body. Not just as a thought, but as a sensation. Let it expand through your chest. This simple practice can transform even the most challenging circumstances.

Every day gratitude lifted my energy, reminded me that life is amazing, and that I was amazing too. It reminded me that magic is real and even in challenging times when the future is uncertain, there is always something to be grateful for.

I quickly carved out a life in Venice. I felt so in tune with my intuition, I knew exactly what to do at every moment. I felt that everywhere I landed was where I was supposed to be. I could feel the truth of my soul beginning to emerge, I could start to feel who I was buried underneath the layers of societal conditioning and beneath the layers I had placed upon myself. I began to feel real joy in my life and equanimity in my mind. I ended up exactly where I was meant to be and every challenge, including Chad's legal problems, was part of the greater plan of my life.

Two months after we landed in LA, Chad and I decided to get married. This may have been my most loyal act ever or my most questionable. But I did it. I did it because I loved him. I did it because at the time, it felt like the best decision.

We called our families with less than a week's notice and somehow, they all made it happen. My parents, Chad's parents and sisters, and even the same friend who had been with me the day I received that fateful voicemail from Chad. They all flew out to support us. The sudden urgency of our wedding plans raised eyebrows, but our families showed up without too many questions. This wasn't exactly the wedding any of them had imagined for us, but they came to support us.

I found a pink cocktail dress on Main Street in Santa Monica after discovering that no wedding shop could deliver a dress in less than three days. It wasn't a traditional wedding gown, but it felt right for this unconventional union. We drove to Vegas through the desert, watching the landscape shift from coastal California to arid Nevada, the reality of what we were doing settling over us with each passing mile.

The ceremony took place at the Flamingo Hotel, a burst of neon pink in the desert that somehow seemed appropriate for our situation—bright, a bit gaudy, and completely unexpected. As I walked toward Chad with our families watching, I felt the weight of everything that had brought us to this moment, including the federal investigations, the uncertainty, and the constant vigilance. But I also felt something else: a strange certainty that this was exactly where I needed to be and that all of it was part of my greater life plan.

The truth was, I loved Chad deeply and would have done anything for him. But I knew our marriage wouldn't last. Not because of his legal troubles, but because I was finally discovering who I really was. As I grew into myself, I could see the disconnect: We loved each other, yes, but we weren't meant to walk the same path. Our hearts connected, but our souls were headed in different directions.

We got married without any expectations, without a honeymoon, and without a long-term plan of any kind. Sometimes you just have to do what feels right in the moment.

The next two years flew by. We lived in the same sublet apartment, making it our own. I studied human anatomy, Chinese medicine, yoga, and meditation, immersing myself in studies to fill my days. I practiced meditation every morning and yoga every afternoon; some of the greatest yoga teachers in the country at the time were within blocks of me. I was grateful to sit with them and soak up their wisdom.

I began teaching yoga once I felt safe enough to put my name on a public list. The Feds continued their investigation, subpoenas kept coming, and the threat of chaos always lingered. But I learned not to let it consume me. Through daily yoga and meditation, I became so attuned to my body and mind that I could catch anxiety before it spiraled. I learned to recognize the subtlest signals; a shift in my breath, tension in my shoulders, or any change that warned me my thoughts were about to take a dark turn. When those thoughts approached, I simply told them no.

To develop this awareness for yourself, start tracking your triggers. Notice when racing thoughts typically begin. Do they show up after scrolling your phone? During difficult conversations? In crowded spaces? Then tune in to your body's early warning system. What physical sensations arise just before your mind starts to spiral? Perhaps your chest tightens, your breathing becomes shallow, or your stomach knots up.

Once you recognize these signals, create a pattern to break them before they get out of control. This could be a specific breathing pattern, touching your thumb to your forefinger, or a simple no. Have a tool ready to redirect your energy, whether it's a gratitude practice, sensory awareness of your surroundings, or physical movement. Strengthen these patterns through consistency. You train your energy, mind, and body to do them at the slightest sign of anxious thoughts. This consistent practice is what allowed me to recognize the first hints of anxiety before they became a full-blown storm.

When thoughts of the Feds taking me or Chad arose, I refused to indulge them. I wouldn't let them spiral into endless "what if" scenarios. I had every reason to imagine the worst. And I had enough fuel to spend my days in an anxious whirlwind, losing touch with my center, my peace, my magic. Instead, I made a conscious choice. I let thoughts flow through my mind like clouds passing overhead, just as meditation had taught me. They came, they went, and I didn't chase them.

Through the two years of waiting for the unthinkable to happen, I managed to create a life that resonated with my soul and to cultivate a sense of inner peace in the unknown. I was transforming from the inside out, finding myself over and over again. I was living in the space in between the old version of myself and the new. It was filled with uncertainty but also limitless potential.

Throughout this time, I learned to completely detach from control and understand that there are things in life that I have to accept. I learned to live fully in the present moment with no attachment to the future. I flowed with my life because I had no choice. I couldn't force anything to happen nor did I want to. All I could do was show up for myself each day fully present and live the reality in front of me.

I also began to slowly dissolve my ego. I didn't intend to do this or even try to, it was just a natural byproduct of the life I was living, a life of uncertainty where the only thing keeping me together was a deep meditation practice.

The ego in spirituality is often called the "false self." It's the part of us that identifies with our thoughts and feelings, meaning if we have a thought, we think we are that thought. Really, we are the person behind that thought. Same for our emotions. If we experience anxiety, for example, our ego might tell us that we are an anxious person. It makes that feeling part of our identity. When really, we are the person having an anxious thought or feeling, not the feeling itself.

As I immersed myself in a land beyond my thoughts and feelings, all my past definitions of myself began to dissolve. I could not live by labels because at the time everything was so uncertain I wasn't sure any label would stick for very long. I gave up on defining myself by my career, what I had accomplished, or what I was going to accomplish. I had barely any possessions and felt no need to accumulate more because they might end up in storage or be taken at any point.

During this time, I made up my mind that there were only four things in life I needed to do every day: meditate, practice yoga, read, and write. I lived with these four things guiding each day. I awakened each morning to meditate with the rising sun. Then I would journal. Some days I would write a stream of consciousness to clear out the fear or anxiety. Other days I would write about what I was understanding and integrating through my practices.

I remember one particularly challenging morning. I had woken from a nightmare about federal agents breaking down our door, my heart still racing as I sat on my meditation cushion. My mind kept replaying the dream images, calculating escape routes, spinning up worst-case scenarios. For twenty minutes, I just kept returning to my breath, over and over, sometimes having to physically place my hand on my chest to feel the rhythm of my heartbeat. By the thirtieth minute, something shifted. My breathing deepened, my shoulders relaxed, and I felt a profound sense of "okayness" wash over me. Not complete peace, but a return of a familiar mantra. In this moment everything is okay.

Later that day, I went to a yoga class where the teacher focused on heart-opening poses. As I moved through backbends and chest expansions, I felt the residual fear from my nightmare melting away. That evening, I read a passage in a book by Pema Chödrön, an American-born Buddhist, about embracing uncertainty, words that seemed written specifically for me in that moment. Before bed, I wrote three pages about finding freedom within confinement, the words coming from somewhere beyond my thinking mind. As I wrote them, I felt like I was not just writing, I was channeling universal knowledge.

This simple rhythm—meditate, move, read, write—carried me through days when nothing else made sense.

This routine saved me from what could have been the most nerve-wracking part of my life. It took a deep commitment. It was hard to stick with it but also empowering. I was deciding my life one day at a time even in uncertainty.

Changing your life begins with one step: the decision to change. That willingness and declaration to yourself propels you forward, even when you don't know your destination. Your intuition awakens and guides you to exactly what you need. This may come in the form of guides, teachers, courses, books, or even new places to visit. Just be willing. Be willing to change your life and everything else will follow.

There was some pain involved in my transformation. I was the butterfly struggling to break out of the cocoon and fly. I felt in the dark much of the time, not knowing when I would break free of the constant pressure. I also didn't know who I would be on the other side. The caterpillar has no idea what it will look like once it finally emerges; it simply trusts the process.

I had to release everything I thought I was or would become. I had to accept that my future might involve a prison cell. I hadn't been charged with breaking any laws, but I did fear the Feds would arrest me as a pathway to Chad and the rest of his clan. It was a real possibility I lived with each day, but I did not allow it to overtake my life. I did know that if I ended up behind those bars, I would meditate, do yoga, read, and write. But all in all, I really wanted to remain free. Every day that I had my freedom, I was grateful. Even when I was sitting in the 405 traffic, I was happy that at least I wasn't in jail. I was free to sit in traffic.

Chad and I were happy in our one-bedroom sublet apartment on the beach for so long that we began to feel comfortable. We began to forget that there was a reason we didn't have utilities in our name, and the only mail we received went to a mailbox down the street. We began to forget the clouds of darkness were still hanging just out of sight, ready to ruin our sunny California day.

Chapter Ten
THE HEART WANTS WHAT IT WANTS

December 2011. I went to yoga that morning to study with the great Maty Ezraty, the founder of YogaWorks. I was doing a weeklong immersive study in Ashtanga yoga. Chad went off to the farmers market and to do whatever he did to fill his days. I wasn't in the habit of asking. We both returned around the same time to our apartment building. There was a strange energy around us. Quickly and quietly, one of our neighbors came up to us and let us know that DEA agents had just been there with the battering ram to break down the door of our apartment.

They didn't get in, and we'll never really know why. We figured it was because we sublet the place, and our name wasn't on the lease. Or maybe it was because I placed an energetic force field of safety around the apartment every morning when I meditated. Every day, I imagined a white light encasing our apartment. It felt safe and I felt protected within it. I would breathe with the light, feeling it expand into a safe cocoon.

Whether it was the white light magic or the legality of the lease agreement, the Feds didn't get in but it was official. Chad had been indicted. We suspected something like this might be on its way because an indictment had come down a few months prior, but all sixteen names on it were sealed, so our lawyers couldn't see them. And then like a warped game of *The Price Is Right*, they were unveiled one by one.

Today, Chad's number was up. His response to this was to grab his go bag from under the bed, which contained his favorite Rolex, some gold coins, a few other things that would be of value in any country, and some clothes. He grabbed his bag and he went.

I felt my heart physically drop in my chest. I had feared this day coming for so long, but somewhere along the way, I had begun to believe we might somehow escape this fate. As he gathered his things, I couldn't bring myself to say a real goodbye. I cried and pretended I would see him soon, acting as though this was just another temporary separation. My heart and mind simply wouldn't let me accept the reality that was unfolding—that this might be goodbye forever. Something deep inside me refused to acknowledge the finality of what was happening. Instead, I clung to a strange hope, a self-protective illusion that this was just one more challenge we would overcome together.

I did not go this time. Chad didn't even ask. He knew I had found my place in life. I had found my people. I had found where I belonged, and it wasn't on the run with him. It was on the Westside of Los Angeles. I was ready to face whatever was about to show up at my door. I would not run from it. I would breathe through it. I would rely on my tools and I would trust my life path. I knew with every fiber in my being I was meant to be right where I was, and whatever was about to come my way would eventually make me into who I was meant to be. I had no fear.

Knowing all of this with unshakable confidence did not make the choice to stay easy. In a matter of moments, I lost one of the greatest loves of my life. Because I did really love him, and the heartache that ensued after his swift departure was real. I began to learn how to mourn the living. Chad didn't die that day but, in a way, he did. And so did our marriage, our life together, and any future we could've ever had. It all died, and the only thing I could do was sit on the floor and sob hysterically for what felt like days.

My ability to live in full presence with myself made it so I was aware of all the emotions that came over me. There was no avoiding them. There was no distraction technique I could use. The more I breathed, the more I cried. The pain overwhelmed me. The heartache immediately hit the core of my being and took over my reality. I was devastated. And I had no idea how I was going to pick myself up.

We don't talk enough about the grief that follows the right decisions. Even when your intuition is clear, even when you know in your soul what path you must take, your heart may still break. It's not a sign that you've chosen wrong. It's just part of being human.

A few people helped me save myself during this time, and I'll forever be grateful to them. Over the previous years, I had managed to make quite a few good friends, even though most of them had no idea of my reality or the uncertainty I was living through daily. I kept those details of my life to myself for fear that anyone who knew my whole story might end up with a subpoena at their door like everyone else we had known. My friends were there for me, though, when I needed them the most.

I remember a friend coming over just a few days after Chad left because she hadn't heard from me, and she was worried. She found me in a crumpled ball on my floor. Instead of asking what was wrong, she simply held me. I didn't want to explain to anyone what was happening. I couldn't find the words. I didn't have the energy to give them the backstory, but luckily, I had some people in my life who could just be present with me and then force me to get some vegan curry down the block because I hadn't eaten in days.

I had enrolled in yoga teacher training and started that same month. It was somewhere my intuition had led me, and I'm so glad it did because it helped me slowly find my power again and reclaim the life I was building. It would take time for the shock waves to dissipate, though, and it would be years until my heart healed. In the first weeks after Chad left, I woke up every day and I felt an iron weight on me. Every day I woke up to the shock of him being gone, and every day I felt like I had to start from the beginning, picking myself up one piece at a time.

This is when I discovered the crucial difference between heart and soul. We're always told to "follow your heart," and usually that's good advice. But not this time. My heart ached to be with Chad. It wanted to run with him, to stop the pain, to feel loved again. My soul knew better. It understood that my path was in California, not on the run. I was meant to walk through this fire, not flee from it.

Ideally, our heart and soul align and then life choices become clear. They may be challenging but they are clear. I found myself in a dilemma of which internal compass to follow. Without much question, I walked in the direction of my soul. At the end of the day, it's our soul's path we're here to walk. I reminded myself that if I kept just doing my four things—meditating, practicing yoga, reading, and writing—I could get through anything. I could get through this heartache. The tears would eventually dry.

Although my heart told me every morning to pack my own go bag and run, I chose my soul and my intuition that told me to stay in my small apartment with the iron weight on my chest waking me up to the reality I was living.

Learning to distinguish between these different internal voices is a skill, one that gets stronger with practice. Here's how you can begin to recognize and work with these different aspects of yourself:

Heart intelligence manifests as a longing or desire, a magnetic pull toward something or someone that feels so strong it creates a physical pull in your chest. This intelligence can be influenced by our attachments and our desires, especially when we're faced with difficult choices. The heart naturally focuses on connection and relationships; it will choose to feel connected even when that connection isn't the right energy for our life's path.

Soul wisdom, by contrast, arrives as a knowing rather than a desire. The heart pulls us, the soul guides us. The soul has a distinctly different quality. It feels like a certainty that remains steady even when emotions flood our consciousness. Your soul naturally takes the long view of your life path, seeing the entire timeline of your life and even your future lives. This wisdom often asks you to step into discomfort for the sake of growth, guiding you toward experiences that may challenge you but ultimately shape you into who you're meant to be. The heart can support this path, but if your evolution requires you to disconnect from someone you love then your heart and soul disagree.

If you find yourself in a similar dilemma, trying to choose between what your heart wants and what your soul knows is right, remember that both voices deserve attention. Both are valid. But when they conflict, knowing which to follow requires a deep connection with your intuition. Your intuition will always know what to do if you trust it enough to listen.

Navigating the conflict between heart and soul requires developing specific practices that bring clarity from your intuitive guidance. You need to connect with your Higher Self, the part of you that knows your life path. Create space to listen to both heart and soul. Then ask your Higher Self for guidance on choosing which to follow.

Pay attention to how these different parts of yourself feel in your body. Try projecting yourself forward in time by imagining yourself five years in the future having made each possible choice. Which future version of yourself feels more aligned, more at peace, more like who you truly want to become? Throughout this process, honor both voices. They both offer powerful wisdom. Even if you ultimately choose to follow your soul over your heart, acknowledge the validity of your heart's desires. Don't shame yourself for wanting what you want, even if you choose something else.

On top of all the heartache, I also had the Feds sitting outside my building every day. They were there in a black Suburban just like in all the movies. Lucky for them, though, I lived on the beach, so they had an amazing view of the ocean while they waited. They were probably biding their time until Chad came back to me, which he didn't. So, they just sat there. When I left home, they followed me around, so I took very long routes to many locations just so they would sit in traffic a bit longer. I had to do something to amuse myself during what seemed like an obscene time in my life.

In graduate school I had studied fear conditioning and, subsequently, deconditioning. I would train mice to associate stimuli with certain consequences, activating their fight-or-flight response. I used my knowledge of fear conditioning to help ease my nerves at the sight of the Feds sitting outside my building. When I returned, I would grab a piece of rosemary from the bush by my door. The scent of rosemary lowers stress and anxiety. I inhaled as I gazed at the black Suburban, training my nervous system to feel relaxed at the sight of it.

I remember one day walking home from yoga, feeling like the 90-minute practice hadn't worked to calm my anxious mind. My thoughts were still racing, my shoulders still tight with tension despite all the downward dogs and forward folds. As I approached my building and saw the familiar black SUV, my heart started its usual acceleration. But then I reached for the rosemary, crushed it between my fingers, and brought it to my nose. It was remarkable, like every pose of the practice suddenly completed itself in that moment. I could feel the relief washing through me, my racing thoughts slowing, the tension melting from my body. It was as if my nervous system had created a new pathway, bypassing the fear response and going straight to calm.

We are so powerful that we can even control our nervous system rather than fighting it. When we face ongoing stressors, we can either remain in a constant state of fight-or-flight, or we can train our bodies to respond differently.

There are practical ways to regulate your nervous system during challenging times that anyone can use. Like my rosemary trick, you too can find sensory experiences that help your body feel safe. Certain scents, textures, sounds, or tastes can become powerful cues for your nervous system. Try creating deliberate associations by pairing the stressor (for me, the sight of federal agents) with something calming (the scent of rosemary). Over time, your body will begin to respond differently to the trigger.

Your breath is always available and can't be taken from you, making it your most constant companion. Simple practices like box breathing, deepening your exhale, or belly breathing can regulate your nervous system in moments of intense stress.

Finding humor wherever possible is also helpful to reduce stress. Even in my stressful circumstances, I found amusement in taking the agents on long drives through traffic. Finding small moments of lightness, even in darkness, is its own form of survival.

Establishing routines that ground you can also help when facing uncontrollable stress. My "four things"—meditating, practicing yoga, reading, and writing—became the center of my Universe. Consider what simple practices could become your nonnegotiables in times of upheaval.

The Feds ultimately served me with a subpoena at the yoga studio where I was teaching, in an attempt to have me reveal Chad's whereabouts. I raised my marital right along with invoking the Fifth Amendment, the right to not incriminate ourselves. It turns out you must raise these rights in person. So, I found myself back in the federal courthouse in Maryland. After some negotiations with my lawyer, they managed to get me into a small room at a table with two federal prosecutors, a DEA agent, an IRS agent, and my lawyer.

The room felt smaller than it was, like the walls were gradually closing in on me with each passing minute. Everything about the space felt oppressive—the flickering fluorescent lights, the musty smell of old files, the hard metal chair digging into my back. I could see in the prosecutors' eyes that they thought they would be able to get more out of me. They seemed genuinely surprised by my unfazed appearance as I sat there, breathing deeply, centering myself despite the pressure.

The whole scene felt stale and colorless, the complete opposite of my life in California. It was as if I had stepped into a different reality altogether, where everything existed in bureaucratic shades of gray. It looked like a scene out of a movie. And like the black Suburban waiting outside my apartment building, it felt very predictable.

One of the prosecutors leaned forward in that cramped room. It would be in my best interest, she said, to tell them everything about Chad's whereabouts. He was now officially indicted, officially a fugitive. If I made any attempt to help him—any attempt at all—they'd charge me with aiding and abetting. But I wasn't helping him. I had no idea where he was. So, I sat there, unmoved by their threats, and silently repeated my mantra: *So Hum, So Hum, So Hum.* For thirty minutes, those two words keep me centered.

I could feel my heart racing, my palms sweating as the prosecutor told me that if Chad loved me as much as I loved him, he would want me to tell them everything I knew. He would want me to save myself and take a plea deal. My lawyer reminded me that I was not charged with anything so there was no plea deal to work out. I just sat there and meditated. I barely remember what they all said. I knew that the best thing I could do for myself was to remain calm. I had the tools to keep myself centered in the moment, and this was my greatest test in using them.

When you face intimidating situations, whether it's federal agents or a difficult boss or a challenging family member, the ability to remain centered is your greatest power. Maintaining your center when everything around you feels chaotic starts with having a go-to mantra or phrase. *So Hum* (I am That) was mine. It could be anything that grounds you—a favorite quote, even just "I am safe, I am here."

I could have been mad at the Feds or even scared into cooperation. I was neither. I knew my rights, I knew I hadn't legally done anything wrong, and I knew I just needed to stay calm enough to get out of that courthouse. They were just doing their job, which was trying to uphold the law. I had the tools to keep my mind and energy calm as I sat there in a tiny room that felt like it was caving in on me with flickering lights and shelves of files, probably filled with criminal cases just like my husband's.

I didn't end up speaking a word to the Feds, nor did I end up testifying. I walked out of the courtroom and once I was far enough away, I screamed. I screamed to shake off the stress. I screamed to release the pain. I screamed to feel my power and I screamed because that's what I needed to do. My lawyer looked at me like I was crazy.

When I arrived back in California, I knew I would never leave. Los Angeles was my home, and no matter what I had to face to remain there, my energy would help me through. My intuition would guide me. I had everything I needed to overcome the challenges in front of me.

And there were more. There was always more. Shortly after getting back to California, the person we sublet the apartment from called and told me he would be evicting me within three days.

He was tired of the Feds harassing him, so he kicked me out. I had nowhere to go because I couldn't get a lease for fear that if I put an apartment in my name on paper it was sure to get raided. So, as I packed up my things again, I reminded myself that I had practices that would guide me and I had friends who would help me. Most importantly, I would figure this out, just as I had figured out everything before this point. And once again I repeated the mantra *So Hum* as I packed.

I had been in that apartment for more than two years. It felt like home. The first real home I'd had since this whole ordeal began. Now I found myself, once again, alone with boxes and uncertainty. There wasn't nearly as much to pack this time, but as I wrapped each item, a different emotion began to surface. Anger. Not just at the situation, but at myself. I realized that Chad always left me holding the bag— literally and figuratively. He would disappear, and I would be the one left to clean up, to pack up, to explain, to deal with the aftermath.

As I taped up another box, the question crashed through me: What was I doing with my life? Why was I living like this? Moving from crisis to crisis, always reacting to circumstances rather than creating them? Heartbreak aside, something had to give. I couldn't keep doing this to myself. I couldn't keep living in this constant state of uncertainty, waiting for the next crisis. I knew I needed to make some fundamental changes and get my life together—not for Chad, not for anyone else, but for me.

Making changes "for me" was a phrase I had to repeat often, like a mantra I was still learning to believe. But this time was different. I had gained real skills to back up the words. I could get through anything because I was amazing and I had proof. The practices I'd learned were powerful. My ability to calm my mind, steady my energy, and stop the downward thought spirals before they began—all through my breath—these practices had proved themselves time and time again. They showed me how amazing I was.

And you too are amazing. Not despite your challenges but including them. Not after you've overcome them, but right in the middle of them. Your amazingness isn't waiting for you on the other side of difficulty. It's available right now as the very resource that will carry you through. You can save yourself from whatever reality you are living by choosing differently. Yes, it might be a struggle to get through the mud of change, but you have the power to create any life you want. You just need to wake up to the one you've already created and decide where and how to change it.

When everything seems to be falling apart, remembering your power becomes essential for survival. Start by speaking to yourself with genuine compassion. Notice how I reminded myself that I had resources, including friends, tools, and my power. But what if you don't have these things yet? Your most powerful resources are already within you: your breath (free and always available), your ability to observe nature with your senses, and your capacity to choose one thought over another. If you lack money, start with what costs nothing. Journal with a piece of paper, practice a walking meditation, or sit quietly for five minutes. Even if you lack connections with people who can support you, become your own friend. When your inner critic gets loud, deliberately speak to yourself as you would to a friend who was facing the same situation.

Look for evidence of your resilience by reminding yourself of previous challenges you've overcome. You already possess powerful evidence of your strength. Focus your attention on what you can control in the situation. I couldn't control the Feds or my landlord, but I could control my breath, my attention, and my next steps.

Practice acknowledging both the challenge and your capacity simultaneously; saying "This is hard *and* I can handle it" is far more empowering than either toxic positivity or defeatism. Also, don't underestimate the power of physical movement to shift your energy. My scream outside the courthouse was an emotional release and a physical act that shifted my energy. Like a dog shaking off his fear after an attack, my scream allowed me to release some of the fear I was holding. What we do with our bodies can shift our minds and can remind us that we are in control of how we feel.

Feeling stronger than I had ever felt, I packed everything and called a friend. I'd kept her in the dark about my situation. I'd kept everyone in the dark, choosing to walk through this hell alone rather than involve anyone else. But she was intuitive and sensed I was in trouble. When I told her I needed a place to stay, she immediately invited me into her beautiful home.

This began my nomadic chapter, moving between the homes of friends who appeared in my life exactly when I needed them most. Sometimes miracles come in the form of open doors and spare couches, in friends who ask no questions but offer exactly what you need. The Universe has a way of placing angels in human form along our path, showing up precisely when we're about to break.

These friends who sheltered me during those dark months did more than just offer a place to sleep, they became witnesses to my resurrection. They saw me at my lowest, yet they held space for my healing with such grace. They made coffee on mornings when I couldn't face the day. They shared their dinner tables when I needed company. And they somehow knew when to let me be and when to pull me back into the world of the living. Their acts of kindness helped me piece myself back together. The people I met on my journey proved that while we must save ourselves, we don't have to do it alone.

Asking for help is not weakness. It's an act of courage. It takes tremendous strength to be vulnerable enough to say, "I need support." Building your own network of angels begins with connecting with one trusted person. You don't need a large circle. Sometimes just one person who can fully see you with empathy is enough to begin the process of healing.

Sharing our whole story can feel overwhelming, but smaller truths like "I'm having a hard time" or "I could use some company" feel manageable. We also must be willing to look beyond obvious sources of support; in my experience, help often comes from unexpected places. The person who becomes your rock might not be your oldest friend or closest family member, but someone who appears in your life at precisely the right moment.

In times of stress, we also need to cultivate the ability to receive gracefully. Many of us find it easier to give help than to receive it, but practice accepting support with gratitude rather than guilt. And remember that allowing others to help you is offering them a gift as well.

Through it all, trust your intuition about who is safe with your vulnerability. Not everyone deserves access to your deepest truths. Notice how your body feels around different people. Tension or relaxation can be important signals about who creates genuine safety for you during difficult times.

I found a new life that involved a lot of couch surfing but also involved the Feds leaving me alone. I had stood up to them. I had gone to their courthouse. I had not told them a thing, and I had my lawyer call them afterward to ask what their intentions were with me. If they weren't going to charge me, then they needed to leave me alone. After almost three years, they finally left me alone.

Looking back now, I see that I had won something far more valuable than what I'd lost. I won my freedom, not just from surveillance but from the need for certainty. I won peace of mind that came from a deeper place than external security. On paper, I had nothing: no home, no clear future, no guarantees. But I had discovered something more essential: I was resilient. I could get through anything. I had my breath, my practice, my fierce determination to stay present. I had friends who showed up without questioning why. Most importantly, I had my power. And I knew I could use that power to create my life—the life I was born to live.

This is where I learned what would later become one of my most quoted insights: *Your greatest magic will come in times of darkness when you have no choice but to trust your own power.*

But you have to be brave enough to trust that you will find the light again. If you just keep believing in yourself, in your resilience and your power, you will find your way out. I had to believe that every piece of my journey—the heartbreak, the fear, the sleepless nights, the unexpected kindnesses, even the gratitude that somehow bloomed in the darkest moments—was leading me home to myself.

If you're facing your own moment of uncertainty or darkness, know that you are more resilient than you could ever imagine. Awaken to your own resilience and trust that you will be able to get through whatever it is that you're facing. Your resilience is already within you. It's not something you need to create or find. It's already part of you, waiting to be remembered and felt. You've already used it when you've faced your fears or when you've allowed yourself to feel pain. Your resilience is activated every time you take a breath even though you think you can't. It's always with you.

When going through times of uncertainty, start by acknowledging what you're actually feeling, without judgment or attempts to push it away. Name your emotions: "This feels really hard" or "I'm not sure I can get through this." This simple act helps place a container around your emotions so you can hold them. In that holding you'll feel stronger. They won't consume you and you'll be able to say to yourself, "I know it feels like I won't make it through this *and* I believe I can." Or "I'm not sure what tomorrow will bring *and* I know I'll figure it out."

Change happens when we acknowledge what is real and true to us while also affirming our power, strength, and resilience. It's not about avoiding what is real but holding it and seeing it as a part of us that needs to be heard while another part—the resilient part—can give it strength.

The more resilient we feel, the more we can face our fears and start to change our life, because we trust that if everything falls apart, we can survive. Better yet, we can find our way home to our truth, to our center, to our strength.

Remember this above all: You have the power to choose your path, even when external circumstances seem to limit your options. You have the wisdom to navigate complexity, even when the way forward isn't clear. You have the strength to face whatever comes, even when you feel like breaking. And you have the resilience to rebuild, no matter what falls apart. This is your life. Your journey. Your adventure. And you are equipped with everything you need to walk it with grace, courage, and even joy—despite the tears that may come.

Chapter Eleven
PAIN IS INEVITABLE, SUFFERING IS OPTIONAL

The next two years following Chad's disappearance were simultaneously the hardest and most magical of my life. They were filled with coincidences, serendipity, and friends who appeared exactly when I needed them. They were also filled with late nights, one-night stands, and all-day hangovers. Yes, I had my spiritual tools and practices, but I also had a fierce desire to numb the pain in my heart, and I was no stranger to methods of escape.

When you're going through trauma, your mind becomes a dangerous and unpredictable place. Yet there I was, night after night, wandering it. Despite all my meditation practice, despite knowing better, I found myself drawn to anything that could quiet the constant chorus of fears and regrets playing in my head. I'd wake up in strange beds after nights of drinking. I'd drag myself to my favorite coffee shop, ordering extra shots of espresso to combat the hangover, all while telling myself this would be the last time. It never was.

That's the thing about self-destruction—it doesn't announce itself. It sneaks into your life often disguised as coping mechanisms that seem perfectly reasonable at the time. One glass of wine to unwind becomes a bottle. A casual flirtation becomes a pattern of seeking comfort and escape in the arms of strangers. What starts as "just tonight" becomes every night, until you can barely remember what it felt like to face your feelings without something to dampen the pain.

I had chosen to stay in Santa Monica to follow my soul's path, yet here I was doing everything possible to escape myself. I feared putting down roots anywhere, kept my commitments low, and lived with one foot in my life and another on the run. This uncertainty ate away at me like acid, corroding the foundation of self-trust I had worked so hard to build.

I realized there were two types of uncertainty living inside of me. The first kind I had learned to embrace; it felt expansive as I let go of control and followed my soul's decision to stay in Los Angeles. This uncertainty asked me to trust and surrender to my path, allowing the unknown to unfold. I had found a strange type of comfort here. The second type of uncertainty was different. This came from the fear and self-doubt about my choice. It resulted in me refusing to fully inhabit my own life, for fear it would get ripped away.

You might think that someone with years of spiritual practice would be immune to such patterns. That somehow all those hours on the meditation cushion would protect me from the allure of self-sabotage. But trauma has a way of dismantling our practices and strategies of peace, leaving us raw and reaching for whatever we can grasp to silence what hurts.

Most people think rock bottom is a place you hit suddenly, like a crash landing. I found it was more like a slow descent, each step taking me further away from myself and my power. I would tell myself I was just letting loose, just having fun, just doing what anyone would do in my situation. I'd convince myself I was handling it, even as my life increasingly revolved around the next escape. I was still functional. I still made it to yoga classes, still showed up for friends, still maintained the outer appearance of having it together. But inside, I was shattering.

I watched myself go through this descent with a kind of detached fascination. Part of me—the part that still remembered who I really was—knew I was spiraling. But another part, the part running from pain, didn't want to stop. Because stopping meant feeling, and feeling meant facing not just the loss of Chad, but the overwhelming uncertainty of my entire life. It meant acknowledging that I had no home, no clear future, and I might have just ruined my life.

In the space of running from myself, the normal rhythms of life felt impossible. I still didn't feel safe enough to put down real roots. Or maybe I was so addicted to the fear that I couldn't possibly imagine living without it. I also didn't know who I was without Chad. I had been with him for over a decade, since I was twenty-three. I couldn't remember what it was like to live outside the drama of his life. This new reality felt strange, I hadn't found my place, and my heart was broken. A pain I just wanted to run from.

I found running from the pain was a full-time job and it never really worked. The pain just followed me around. The very things I did to escape my suffering became their own source of suffering. The hangovers got worse, the empty encounters left me feeling hollower, and underneath it all, the pain I was running from was still there, waiting patiently for me to come home to myself and realize my power to heal it.

Not only would I have to heal my heartache, I would have to heal the part of me that was wired for a life of fear. And I would have to define who I was now. Who I was without Chad and who I would become.

Healing often comes in unexpected forms. For me, it began in a small yoga studio where people gathered to chant ancient Sanskrit mantras.

My yoga mentor and friend, Sara Ivanhoe, brought me there. She was leading me through the yoga training I had signed up for just before Chad left. She didn't know my whole story, no one did at the time, but she sensed I was in trouble. She didn't judge me, she didn't question me, she just helped me. She knew I needed something beyond the traditional yoga classes, so as part of my teacher training assignments, she sent me to study Kirtan yoga, otherwise known as devotional chanting. Kirtan is part of an ancient form of yoga known as Bhakti, or the Yoga of Devotion.

I stumbled into the Bhakti Yoga Shala in Santa Monica one evening, still slightly hungover. Sara had insisted that I meet her there. That night opened the pathway for healing that would eventually lead me home to myself.

Night after night, I would sit on the wooden floor among strangers who would become friends, letting the vibrations of mantras wash over me as tears streamed down my face. There was something powerful about the presence of Krishna Das, a Grammy-nominated Kirtan singer in a room, his voice rising from a few feet away, as a hundred hearts joined to sing in sync with him as he played the harmonium. In those moments of collective devotion, I could feel my connection to the Universe again, and it was holding me in my pain.

I would sit there, chanting, and feel connected to everything. I would feel connected to Chad, wherever he was, connected to the past version of myself, and even the future me who had made it through all this pain. Most importantly, I felt connected to my heart. I could access it again after shutting it off for so long. I had turned away from my heart as a survival mechanism. I couldn't trust it for so long. As I chanted, though, I opened my heart again. I allowed myself to feel its grief. And somewhere in that pain, I could start to feel my joy again. It was a small seed, but it was there, ready to bloom into something that I could trust.

The magic of Kirtan is that it bypasses the thinking mind and goes straight to the heart. When we chant, we're not just making pretty sounds. We're engaging in a practice that's been used for thousands of years to connect with something larger than ourselves. In those hours of devotional singing, I began to experience what the ancient texts call "nondual awareness," a state where the illusion of separation dissolves and you realize your fundamental oneness with all that is.

As my voice joined with others, as the rhythms of the mantras synchronized our hearts, I could feel my individual pain being held in a much larger container of universal love. I wasn't alone in my suffering. I was part of a vastness that is the human experience, where we are all connected in our joy, sorrow, and love with the Universe. We are all threaded together and interconnected. We are never alone.

The more I chanted, the more my heart began to open. And as it opened, I found something surprising: Alongside my pain lived an incredible power. I began to understand that I didn't need to numb my pain to survive it. I could feel it fully, let it move through me, let it teach me what it had come to teach.

One night, Govindas, one of the regular Kirtan leaders at the Shala, told me something I'll never forget: "Your pain is not a punishment. It's an initiation." He explained that in many spiritual traditions, the heart breaking open is seen as a necessary step on the path to awakening. It's through our brokenness that we discover our wholeness. As our heart breaks open, it opens us to our connection to everything in the Universe. Our perspective shifts and we can connect to things we may have never realized existed before our heartache.

The more I sat with my pain, the easier it was to bear. Sometimes that meant crying through an entire Kirtan session. Sometimes it meant feeling waves of anger or fear move through my body as the mantras washed over me. But each time I showed up, each time I chose feeling over avoidance, I could sense myself healing at a deeper level.

After months of chanting in the Shala, Sara invited me to the Bhakti Yoga Festival, a gathering in the desert of thousands of people to practice yoga and practice Kirtan. The desert was oppressively hot. I could barely breathe, and the yoga rooms were not cooled. I went to workshop after workshop practicing poses, attempting to stay present but wanting to run.

What was I running from? The heat was unbearable, yes, but there was something more threatening: the full presence of my attention on my heart. Each downward dog, each warrior pose threatened to crack me open in ways I wasn't sure I could handle. The practices that were meant to bring presence instead made me want to flee.

After one yoga session, I walked out into the crowd, watching other yogis walk down a path in front of me. I felt so alone, like I was wandering the desert alone with no end in sight. Even surrounded by hundreds of people—people who wouldn't judge me and who would probably have eagerly listened to my story had I told them—I still felt alone.

Just then, I remembered something Chad had told me a long time ago: "You have to trust someone."

I had yet to tell anyone my story. No one, not even my closest relatives knew what I was going through. Partly because I didn't have the strength to tell the tangled tale. Partly because I feared judgment. Partly because I was ashamed of my choices and where I had led my life.

I would later learn from Brené Brown, a shame researcher, that shame grows in the darkness. And the only way to shed light on it is to speak it. We must trust someone with our story to own it, to break the shame that secrecy feeds. I didn't quite understand the intricacies of shame at the time or that I would never find my power if I continued to shame myself. I knew, though, that I had to trust someone.

The Universe, in its perfect timing, presented an opportunity on the drive home. I found myself in a car with Jake, someone who had studied with Ram Dass, a spiritual teacher whose work on presence and consciousness had guided countless seekers. Jake had a gentle presence, a quality of attention that felt safe. Sara had introduced us earlier, mentioning his dedicated spiritual practice, and I knew intuitively that he wouldn't judge or shame me.

So, I did what had seemed impossible just hours before—I spilled everything. During the two-hour drive from the desert back to Los Angeles, with the landscape blurring past the windows and the air-conditioning creating a hum of privacy, I told him my whole story. Every detail about Chad, the federal investigations, the hiding, the fear. I talked about the betrayal, the heartbreak, the countless nights spent numbing myself with whatever was available.

And it felt like resurrection. I physically felt the release of finally sharing my truth with another human being. It felt as if the iron weight that had been crushing my chest every morning finally lifted. I hadn't fully realized how heavy the energy I'd been carrying was until I freed myself from it. Jake listened. He didn't interrupt me. He didn't ask many questions. He just listened with an open heart. After listening, he said something that would permanently shift my perspective: "Pain is inevitable, but suffering is optional."

When I looked at him confused, he explained that pain is what life brings us—the losses, the heartbreaks, the disappointments. But suffering is what we add to that pain with our thoughts, our resistance, our attempts to escape it.

This distinction cracked something open in me. I had been trying so hard to avoid my pain that I'd created an entire additional layer of suffering: the hangovers, the shame, and the disconnection from myself. The pain of losing Chad, of facing an uncertain future, of living with constant fear was unavoidable. But the suffering I'd piled on top of it through my attempts to escape? That was a choice I didn't have to keep making.

"Suffering is optional" became my new mantra. Anytime I would have the urge to run to the bar or to the arms of someone who didn't deserve me, I would remember that I was choosing more suffering. If I could learn to sit with the pain, accept it, and observe it for what it was, the suffering would decrease. The pain of my past would still be there, and honestly still is there today as I write these words. But the pain no longer causes suffering. It also no longer controls or contains me. It's simply part of my story.

The Kirtan community became my holding space for this transformation. Jake introduced me to Lia, who quickly became my best friend. Her presence always reminded me that I wasn't alone. She would become the next person to whom I told my entire story, and it was easier the second time. She didn't make a big deal about it, and after I told her, she said, "We all have a story. It's what we do with that story that matters."

I eventually found the courage to share my past with my mentor, Sara, as well. She brushed it off as though she had already intuited much of it, which wouldn't have surprised me given her perceptiveness. But she offered something invaluable—permission to connect with my anger. One day after Kirtan, she told me that if I was ever to fully heal, I would have to get really angry at Chad and all of his choices. Instead of simply blaming myself and taking responsibility for everything, it would serve me to acknowledge my rage.

Anger, she explained, is an essential stage of healing that many spiritual people try to bypass in their rush toward forgiveness. And while I didn't blame Chad for my current situation, it did feel unexpectedly liberating to get mad at him. I remembered the flash of anger I'd felt on the night of my last move after being kicked out of my apartment. I reconnected with that energy and let it motivate me to change my life.

Anger, when channeled consciously, helped me find my power. It motivated me to stop self-sabotaging myself and change my life one small step at a time. So, I got angry, and let myself feel that anger. And that anger also began to heal me.

In the company of those who could hold my truth without shame or judgment, I began to remember who I was beneath all the layers of trauma and fear. Their witness gave me permission to emerge from the cocoon I'd trapped myself in. My heart would take years to fully mend, but real healing started the moment I trusted someone with my story and owned it as mine.

Along with my Kirtan sessions, I would religiously make it to Erich Schiffmann's yoga class twice a week. The cool wooden floors of Exhale Yoga Shala became another sanctuary, and Erich, though he didn't know it, became one of my most powerful teachers. He would greet me with the same welcoming smile every time. And he had the kindest eyes that instantly made me feel seen and accepted.

Being in Erich's class was like receiving a warm hug from the Universe itself. He had this way of creating space where you could just be—no pretense, no need to hide your struggles, no pressure to be anything other than exactly who you were in that moment. He didn't know anything about my past, the pain in my heart, or the fear that lived in my energy. Yet somehow, his words were always exactly what I needed to hear.

I remember one morning session clearly. With my nervous system humming its usual low-grade anxiety, I settled onto my mat. Erich began one of his characteristic dharma talks. These weren't your typical yoga philosophy lectures. They were more like transmissions of pure universal wisdom, delivered with a casual grace only Erich could pull off.

That day, he dove deep into the concept of enemies. "You have no enemies," he said, his voice carrying that quiet certainty that made you lean in and listen. "Everyone is you, and you are everyone. The person you think is your enemy is just another aspect of yourself, showing you where you need to grow."

The words hit me like lightning. All these months, I'd been carrying the weight of seeing the federal agents as my enemies, as threats to my freedom and peace. I'd been living in a state of constant hypervigilance, looking for danger around every corner. But what if they weren't my enemies at all? What if they were just playing their part in the greater unfolding of my life's path?

Erich went on to explain the fundamental interconnectedness of all beings, how at the deepest level, we're all expressions of the same universal energy. I've always believed this, and Erich reminded me of the truth I had discovered many years ago. A truth that quantum physics is beginning to verify. We're all made of the same stardust, all connected by threads of energy, all playing our roles in each other's awakening.

"When you see someone as your enemy," he continued, "you're creating separation where none truly exists. You're forgetting that they're just another reflection of yourself." He paused, letting that sink in. "And sometimes, the ones who challenge us most are our greatest teachers."

Something shifted in me that day. The federal agents transformed in my mind from threats to teachers. They weren't out to get me. They were playing their necessary part in my soul's evolution. They were pushing me to find my strength and to discover what I was really made of. They were helping me walk the path I was born to walk, even if it didn't feel that way at the time.

This understanding rewired my nervous system. The part of me that had been on high alert for years began to soften. If we were all one universal energy, then there was nothing to defend against. If everyone was me and I was everyone, then even those who seemed to oppose me were ultimately helping me grow.

It also reached deeper than my mind, straight to my heart. As I sat with this truth of universal connection, my heart began to heal in ways

I hadn't expected. Yes, it still ached for Chad, but now I could see even that heartbreak as something placed on my path to help me evolve. The pain wasn't punishment; it was transformation.

Erich's teaching aligned perfectly with what I'd been experiencing in Kirtan at the Bhakti Yoga Shala. The mantras spoke of this same truth, that beneath all apparent separation lies universal connection. But in Erich's class that day, it was being presented in a way that directly addressed my life situation. It wasn't just about feeling connected during chanting; it was about carrying that understanding into every challenging thought that triggered an old fear of being ripped out of my life and thrown into a prison cell.

This simple truth of connectedness began to ripple through my life. If there were no real enemies, then there was no need to keep running, no need to stay in fight-or-flight mode, no need to numb myself with alcohol and casual encounters. I could begin to relax into the understanding that everything—even the difficult parts, especially the difficult parts—was part of my path.

That day in Erich's class marked the beginning of my next phase. As I learned to see everyone as aspects of the same universal consciousness, including those I had feared, my need to escape began to diminish. I could start to trust that everything was unfolding exactly as it needed to for my highest evolution.

The journey through our darkest moments isn't easy, but it teaches us about ourselves in a way that peaceful moments never could. We all have our patterns of self-destruction. Maybe it's not alcohol and casual encounters like mine were. Maybe it's overworking until you burn out, or losing yourself in toxic relationships, or shopping until your credit cards scream, or numbing yourself with endless scrolling on social media. The specific flavor of escape doesn't matter. What matters is recognizing that these patterns aren't character flaws or signs that you're broken. They're survival mechanisms that once served a purpose but now stand between you and your true power.

The first step to transforming these patterns is simply acknowledging them without judgment. This isn't about beating yourself up or adding shame to your energy. It's about bringing awareness to the ways you check out, numb out, or run away when life feels too intense. It's about understanding that whatever your pattern is, it developed for a reason. It was your mind's way of protecting you from pain that felt too big to handle at the time.

But here's what I wish someone had told me: Healing the pain beneath these patterns isn't a straight line. It's more like a spiral. You'll circle back to the same wounds, but each time from a slightly higher vantage point. Your nervous system holds the memory of every heartbreak, every betrayal, every moment that felt like too much. Your body remembers even when your mind tries to forget. And that's okay. That's human.

Small, unexpected triggers can send you tumbling back into old patterns. A song on the radio, a familiar scent, someone's laugh that sounds like theirs, and suddenly you're reaching for whatever used to numb the ache. When this happens, remember: You're not failing. You're not starting over. You're just meeting another layer of healing that's ready to be addressed.

You are so much stronger than your patterns. The very fact that you developed these patterns shows how resourceful you are, how determined your spirit is to survive. And just as you had the power to create these patterns, you have the power to transform them. Your patterns don't diminish your amazingness, they prove it.

The key is to face these patterns with compassion rather than judgment. To understand that every time you drink too much, or shop too much, or lose yourself in whatever your particular escape might be, you're really just avoiding what you *think* needs to be fixed. But you don't need to fix anything. You're not broken. You're human, and humans need time to heal. What you need isn't fixing; it's tenderness. Extra care. The same gentle attention you'd give a physical wound that's still mending.

When you're in the thick of healing, be extraordinarily kind to yourself. Rest more. Move slower. Say no to things that drain you. Ask for help even when your ego insists you should handle it alone. Surround yourself with people who understand that healing happens in waves, who won't shame you for having hard days, who can sit with you in the mess without trying to rush you through it.

And be honest with yourself and know you are strong enough to handle that honesty.

When you're ready to face your patterns, you don't have to do it alone. Find your people—the ones who will hold space for your healing without trying to fix you. Find your practices—the ones that help you stay present even when presence feels uncomfortable. And find your power—it's there, waiting patiently beneath every pattern you've used to hide it.

Awakening isn't about becoming someone new. It's about remembering who you've been all along, beneath the patterns, beneath the pain, beneath the protective layers you've built around your heart. It's about learning to hold yourself through the nonlinear journey of healing, to be patient when old pain resurfaces, to trust that each return to a familiar hurt is actually an opportunity to heal it more deeply.

Every pattern you face becomes a doorway to love, love for yourself. Every demon you acknowledge loses its power to control you from the shadows. And while you still may live with that demon, it no longer tells you what to do; instead you learn to soften it with a hug, a smile, and gentle compassion. Welcome your demons, sit with them, have a conversation with them, make them tea. Only then will you be free of their self-sabotaging ways. And they will have no power over you.

You can face whatever pain or pattern has been running your life. You can look at them directly, understand them deeply, and eventually, transform them completely. Not because you're broken and need fixing, but because you're ready to reclaim the full power while honoring the time and tenderness that true healing requires.

The Universe has a way of bringing us exactly what we need to evolve, even when it comes disguised as our worst nightmare. My patterns led me to life-changing mentors and a deeper understanding of my own strength. Your patterns, whatever they may be, can lead you to your own awakening if you're willing to see them as teachers rather than something to hide.

Start where you are. Notice your patterns without trying to change them yet. Be gentle with yourself as you build awareness. Trust that just as I found my way through the darkness of self-destruction to a place of greater power and purpose, you can too. Because you are, and have always been, absolutely amazing. Your patterns don't define you. They are not who you are. They're just showing you where your next level of growth is waiting to happen.

The same power that created your patterns can transform them. The same heart that's closed off from the world and has been trying to protect itself can learn to open again. The same amazing spirit that's been hiding your stories can share them and feel alive again. All you have to do is be willing to look, to feel, to stay present with whatever arises. And be willing to begin, again and again, with all the compassion you can hold for your beautifully human self.

Your awakening is already happening. Your power is already there. Your amazingness has never left. It's just waiting for you to own it.

Chapter Twelve
IN THIS MOMENT, YOU ARE OKAY

When you think you've faced all your demons, life has a way of introducing you to new ones. In the spring of 2014, just when I thought I had found some stability, the ground shifted again. I was living with my friend, Lia, in Venice, sleeping on a pull-out trundle bed, my collection of crystals the only remnants of my former life. I had made peace with this simplified existence, had even started to find beauty in it. But the Universe wasn't done teaching me yet.

It started with a phone call from my storage unit manager. Something had happened to my lock, he said. His voice had an edge. By now, I was fluent in the language of trouble. I could hear it in pauses, in the careful choice of words, in what wasn't being said. That familiar pit formed in my stomach, the one that had become my constant companion during the years of federal investigations.

I knew better than to let fear paralyze me. When trouble comes knocking, it's better to open the door than to let it break it down. So, I drove the quarter mile to the storage center, willing my dinner to stay down, preparing myself for whatever I might find. The manager's confession came quickly: The DEA had been there. They had cut through my locks, methodically gone through every box, filing cabinet, and couch cushion, leaving chaos in their wake. He handed me a new lock, as if that could secure what had already been breached.

This visit from the DEA made no sense. They had left me alone for years—why now? What had changed? The questions swirled in my mind as I retraced all my steps and conversations over the last two months. I had learned enough about federal investigations to know that timing is rarely random. Someone had given them a reason to dig through my life again.

It was with this weight of an unknown betrayal on my shoulders that I headed to my first Vipassana retreat the following week. Vipassana is a type of meditation that teaches you how to sit with the sensation of the body in full presence. To properly learn this technique, you go to a ten-day silent retreat in an isolated location. No phones, technology, or even eye contact is allowed. The point of the retreat is to mimic being completely alone with absolutely no external influences, to become one with your body, mind, and energy.

I've always called this retreat the "Navy Seals" of meditation training. Vipassana is challenging to say the least. But it breaks the resistance to full present awareness so many of us have. During a ten-day retreat, the only option is to observe every sensation and make peace with it. This includes physical pain, emotional pain, and, for me, it included layers upon layers of residue buildup from a life of questionable choices.

A friend had told me about Vipassana and encouraged me to go. She thought it would help change my life and she was right. I had signed up for the retreat months before the ransacking of my storage unit. The timing, though, was perfect. I thought ten days of silence might help me find some clarity, might help calm the anxiety that had started humming through my nervous system again. I had no idea that this retreat would not just become a lesson in meditation but would lead to understanding the heart of forgiveness.

What most people don't tell you about sitting for days on end is that it hurts. It really hurts. The physical pain was excruciating. I couldn't even get to the emotional pain. The layers waiting to be peeled like an onion were out of reach because all I could do was feel the pain in my hips, legs, back—basically my whole body. I squirmed in the retreat hall on my meditation cushion, searching for the perfect position when there was none. The physical pain was the first sensation I learned to sit and observe. Just like I couldn't control the agents who broke into my storage unit, I could not control the physical pain of sitting. I could only observe it.

Three days into my silence, I started to feel a new sensation in my body, a burst of heat rising up from my sacrum, through my spine directly to the top of my right ear. It was unlike anything I had ever experienced. Perhaps this was another kundalini awakening? The yogic texts always described physical sensations like heat rising up the spine as an unlock of sacred energy held in the sacrum, leading toward a new level of enlightenment or awakening. Had I unlocked something already during my first three days of silence? Was this the grand payoff for all the pain?

No, it wasn't. It was chicken pox. Nothing spiritual or energetic or even mystical. Just plain old chicken pox. Later that night, back in the dormitory, I noticed a spot on my right ear where the heat had erupted and a spot on my belly. Definitely chicken pox. Unsure of what to do, since I wasn't technically supposed to talk to anyone, I just lay in bed practicing the meditation I was learning, trying to make it to dawn.

When the sun finally rose, I filed into the meditation hall with the others as usual. I immediately put my name on the list to speak with one of the teachers, then settled onto my cushion as a thunderous voice filled the space through the speakers, guiding us in morning meditation. The voice belonged to S. N. Goenka, an Indian Vipassana meditation teacher.

As I sat there, I tried to apply the Vipassana technique, scanning my body for clues. Had the meditation somehow unlocked a dormant strain of chicken pox? Was this even possible? My mother had exposed me to every chicken pox–infected kid in my childhood, convinced I was somehow immune when I never caught it. Now, decades later, here it was, making its appearance in the middle of a silent retreat.

During the break, I waited for my turn with the teacher, rehearsing what to say. When I finally entered her chamber, all pretense of a composed meditation student fell away. "I think I have chicken pox," I blurted out.

Her surprised "What?" told me this wasn't the usual type of consultation she handled. Most people came with questions about their meditation technique or seeking validation they were doing it correctly. Not me. Here I was, showing her the spots on my belly and ear, seeking confirmation of a childhood disease.

"I cannot diagnose you," she said, "but I can advise you to consider this a lesson in sitting with uncomfortable sensations. Life will always be full of events we cannot control. Our path is to sit with all sensations and observe them for what they are—sensations neither negative nor positive."

I felt frustration rising in my chest. I understood the spiritual teaching, but this wasn't just about me and my discomfort. "Well, I don't like being here if I have chicken pox. There's a pregnant lady out there," I pointed out.

"Of course, you don't like it," she responded serenely. "You can't control it. Your job is to learn how to accept and be at peace with what you can't control, not control it."

I felt like screaming. Yeah, I got it—this was just another lesson. But seriously? Chicken pox?

Realizing I wasn't going to get practical help here, I thanked her and left, emerging from the dark hall into the bright sunlight in search of someone who worked at the retreat center. I found a young woman and approached her directly: "Hi, I think I have chicken pox, and I'd like to leave. I can't sit through this. I'm not a monk."

She looked skeptical until I showed her my belly. Her doubt transformed instantly into certainty: "Yeah, that's chicken pox. You definitely have to leave. I can't even allow you to stay if you wanted to. I'll escort you to your room to gather your things and unlock your phone from storage."

Just like that, my attempt to find enlightenment was over. Within minutes, I was standing in the parking lot, phone in hand, feeling bewildered, feverish, and unsure of what to do next.

Once in my car, the reality of my situation crashed over me. I was four hours from home, possibly under federal investigation again, and really freaking itchy, like all over, and observing the sensations of each pock as it formed did not help.

I hadn't even learned the proper way to end a Vipassana retreat. They normally did a slow reintegration back into the world of speech and technology. But my life had never followed the normal rules. I was used to sudden shifts, to plans dissolving, to having to think on my feet. So that's what I did.

I pulled into the CVS parking lot, needing to understand exactly what I was dealing with. The fluorescent lights felt harsh after days of gentle meditation hall lighting. I grabbed a thermometer, ibuprofen, and some snacks—the essentials for what was clearly going to be an interesting journey. Back in my car, I waited for the thermometer to beep: 104 degrees. Perfect.

As I examined my ear in the rearview mirror and googled chicken pox images (technology feeling strange in my hands after days without it), a deeper anxiety began to surface. I couldn't just check into a hotel somewhere between here and LA. Not with the DEA suddenly active in my life again. The raid on my storage unit was too recent, too concerning. Every hotel required ID, credit cards, a paper trail I couldn't afford to leave right now.

I called Lia, my friend from the Yoga Shala. We had become close over the years, and I had been crashing at her place—actually my friend Michael's place, where she rented a room. "Well, you can't come here," she said. "I could get shingles from you. You can give people shingles even if they've had chicken pox already."

She was a bit of a hypochondriac, so I didn't argue. I had been staying with her and Michael because I couldn't have my name on a lease at the moment. Having a husband on the run makes things like that a bit challenging. So, I didn't press her.

"Tell me where you end up! I'm worried about you!" she said before we hung up.

Okay, so I was four hours away from LA with chicken pox, had nowhere to go, and couldn't go to a hotel. Still in the parking lot, I closed my eyes again and took a deep breath. I repeated the mantra I told myself every time a challenge arose: "In this moment, I am okay." It had worked for me through a lot and always cleared my thoughts and connected me to the present moment.

I quickly called another friend whom I had frequently stayed with over the years. She always had graciously taken me in. Having been a Vipassana meditator herself for many years, she was more concerned with how quickly I ended the course.

"You need to get somewhere serene and try to finish the course yourself. It's not good for your nervous system to end so abruptly," she warned.

"Well, can I come to your house?" I hopefully asked.

"No," she replied, "my son hasn't had the chicken pox vaccine yet, and I don't want you to give it to him."

Okay, next . . .

I called several friends, one after another. No, no, and no. When had chicken pox become scarlet fever? They all were worried about getting shingles. Which, by the way, is untrue. You can't get shingles from someone with chicken pox. It just doesn't work like that, but no one would believe me.

In the fog of my feverish mind, I had an idea. One of my yoga clients was away in San Francisco for work. He had just told me about the trip last week. I quickly dialed his number. I explained the situation to him (minus the federal surveillance) and asked if I could stay at his house while I recovered. He said of course, and told me where the spare key was hidden.

Excited to have a plan and happy to feel the ibuprofen starting to break the fever, I pulled out of the parking lot and started heading to Hollywood Hills. In his expansive home, I would spend the next week finishing my Vipassana meditation, observing the sensation of each pock as I calmed my nervous system, all while gazing over the city of LA. Serene—check, Fed-free—check, a reminder that I always can figure out any situation—check.

As I sat staring over the Hollywood sign, something clicked. A pattern I'd seen before but hadn't wanted to acknowledge. The timing of the storage unit raid, the specific items they'd gone through, the areas they'd focused on. It wasn't random. Someone had given them information, specific information. Someone who knew where I kept things, who knew my habits, who knew my life. Only a handful of people knew the details of my life that the DEA had seemed interested in. The betrayal, when I finally let myself see it, was breathtaking and far worse than the chicken pox.

One of my friends—the one who had been with me when I had first listened to the voicemail that changed everything—had been feeding information to the federal agents. The realization felt like another fever breaking over me, hot then cold, leaving me shaky and unsure of what was real.

My friend had orchestrated an elaborate betrayal that I wouldn't fully understand until weeks later. The last time I saw them, something felt off, a subtle shift in energy I couldn't quite place at the time. It was only later that I realized they had been trying to get me to say something that would implicate me in aiding and abetting Chad on the run. I had no idea of Chad's whereabouts at the time and simply was focused on my healing journey, so their attempt to set me up failed.

When life throws its most unexpected challenges at you, and it will, your power lies not in avoiding these moments but in how you move through them. We often think strength means never falling down. The truth is, strength is revealed in how we rise from the unexpected.

The storms that seem designed to break us are often the very experiences that teach us what we're made of. Each time I faced a new obstacle—the ransacked storage unit, chicken pox at a meditation retreat, the realization of betrayal—I had a choice: collapse or adapt, surrender to panic or find my center, become bitter or learn to forgive. These weren't easy choices, especially when betrayal came from someone I trusted deeply. Yet how I walked through these choices revealed a capacity for resourcefulness I hadn't known I possessed.

And like I said in the beginning, I'm not a guru or special in any way. You have the same capacity as I do to walk through the fires of your life. You too can turn your struggle into a beautiful journey that gives you wings. You don't need to know all the answers in advance. You just need to trust that when challenges arise, you can figure out your path through them one step at a time. You can save yourself, just as I did. You can even borrow my mantra: "In this moment, I'm okay." Because even in your darkest hour, something within you knows exactly what the next step should be.

And like me, you too can survive life's more heartbreaking events like betrayal and turn them into something meaningful. Every challenge, every betrayal, every heartbreak carries within it the seeds of growth if we're willing to look for them. This doesn't mean pretending the pain isn't real or the injustice doesn't matter. It means refusing to let these experiences have the final say in your story.

In that borrowed house, staring at the hills below, I realized that this betrayal would either break me or break me open. The choice was mine. But sitting there, I began to understand something powerful: When someone betrays you, it forces you to examine every choice that led you to that moment. Who did I trust? What signs did I ignore? Where did I abandon my intuition?

Maybe it was the quiet of the hills, or that my body finally had a moment to really relax despite the chicken pox, but a hard truth began to emerge. I had betrayed myself first. I had silenced my own inner voice when it whispered warnings. I had explained away red flags, ignoring them. I had chosen to trust someone because they had been trustworthy in the past, but now my intuition was warning me that they were no longer trustworthy in this new atmosphere of legal drama.

And though I didn't yet understand how, I knew this experience would eventually lead me toward a deeper understanding of forgiveness, not just of the people in my life but of myself. Because I realized that any anger or betrayal I felt toward them was also anger toward myself for not honoring or at least exploring what my newfound inner voice was trying to tell me. And you can't manifest the life you deserve when carrying the weight of self-betrayal. You can't truly love yourself while living in a sea of regret. You can't create from a place of shame. And at the moment, I felt all of that.

    The forgiveness had to start with me.

Chapter Thirteen
FORGIVENESS IS FREEDOM

Shortly after my chicken pox revelations, I received a letter from the IRS politely informing me they had seized money from me, and if I wanted to prove it was legally mine, I could call them. I did not call them, nor did I confront my friend who betrayed me. Instead, I found myself in my friend Michael's kitchen learning how to bake German chocolate cake while listening to Jefferson Airplane on vinyl. Michael had the most amazing record collection, and the nights spent in his kitchen listening to them healed something within me that had probably been there since childhood.

Michael gave me a soft landing in his home and heart. He lived an eclectic life. A true citizen of Venice beach, his home had an open door. At any point in time, you could find someone just off Burning Man sleeping in a tent in the backyard or a budding herbalist sleeping on the couch. My cousin called his house the quintessential hippie den. I'm not sure if that's the most accurate description, but it was one of the most stable and grounding places for me and many others who were carving out a life that didn't fit into a conventional box.

Lia had invited me to stay in the room she rented in Michael's home while she was in Hawaii a few months back. I immediately felt at home and couldn't bring myself to leave. When Lia returned, we all lived together with a few others who made their way in and out of the house. Lia and Michael taught me how to trust again, how to be present with my grief. They lifted me out of some of my darkest days.

Michael's kitchen was always warm with the smell of something cooking, and it became the place where I began to feel the potential of my future. I would stand in his kitchen, usually in the way but sometimes being of help, talking with him about everything from neuroscience to herbs to stories of Venice Beach in the seventies. I eventually shared my own story with Michael, and he didn't judge me. He simply saw it as another part of the interesting world we all live in.

I still had an overwhelming anxiety that someone would burst through Michael's door and take me away at any moment. One day, though, shortly after the letter from the IRS arrived, when I was sure I was about to be arrested at any moment, I lay down in front of an altar Lia had created with pictures of Indian gurus and statues. I allowed my full body to release into the floor beneath me. I grabbed my nearest crystals and placed them along my body, hoping they would steady my nervous system and anxious thoughts. I then silently declared that I was ready for anything that my path brought me. If I was meant to go to prison, I would figure it out. If I was meant to stay on Lia's floor in Michael's house, I would figure it out. If I was meant to continue teaching yoga or do something else with my life, I would figure it out. I surrendered, completely.

I just didn't want to worry anymore. I wanted to choose something different for my life and energy. I remembered the somewhat annoying

Vipassana teacher's advice about control. I gave up trying to control a situation that I couldn't possibly even know enough about to control. I gave in to my heartbreak for Chad and allowed myself to cry, knowing that falling apart would put me back together again. And I cried about the betrayal that had led me here again, a place I thought I had dug out of. I gave up and surrendered to the Universe's plan for me, knowing that I could always count on myself to navigate any path.

The simple act of surrender in the container of Michael's home shifted something within me. I was able to leave the anxiety behind and begin to find a path forward, out of what felt like minute-to-minute hell and anguish and into a new vibration.

In Michael's kitchen, immersed in measuring, sifting, and washing dishes, I found a different kind of spiritual practice than what I'd sought at Vipassana. You can find meditation in simple acts when you place your full presence in them. He and Lia created space for me to remember who I was beyond all the labels of "suspect," "estranged wife," or "betrayed friend."

A few weeks after my truncated Vipassana retreat, when the chicken pox finally healed, I also got my first tattoo: "This too shall pass" written in my own handwriting on my inner left arm. It wasn't just about the federal agents or the chicken pox or even the betrayal. It was a reminder that everything in life is temporary, both the painful and the beautiful moments. The tattoo became another personal mantra, a permanent reminder of impermanence.

The friend who betrayed me had tried to destroy my life. Instead, their betrayal pushed me further along my path of resurrection. In Michael's kitchen, learning to bake cakes and trust again, I rebuilt myself piece by piece. Sometimes betrayal becomes the doorway to a deeper kind of healing, one that no retreat or journey abroad could have given me.

What makes betrayal so devastating isn't just the act itself, it's how it forces you to question every conversation. How every moment that held meaning becomes tainted by the film of betrayal and pain. The connection you had comes into question. Was any of it real? The mind can create endless possibilities, each one feeling worse than the one before.

I found myself replaying conversations, looking for signs I might have missed. Like the time they had asked detailed questions about my living situation or their sudden interest in my travel plans. The hypervigilance I thought I'd moved past came roaring back. I could have easily started seeing potential betrayal everywhere, questioning every friendship, doubting every kindness. But I caught myself, and having Michael and Lia by my side helped me from tumbling down the familiar path of mistrust.

In Michael's home, I began to understand something about forgiveness. It wasn't about excusing what my friend had done or pretending it hadn't hurt. It wasn't about understanding their reasons or waiting for an apology that would never come.

Forgiveness was about choosing my own freedom over the prison of resentment. I came to learn that forgiveness isn't a single decision but a process with distinct stages. It begins with fully acknowledging the hurt and allowing yourself to feel it completely. For weeks, I let myself feel the full weight of the betrayal, the fear, the anger. I didn't try to bypass these emotions or pretend I was "above" them. This honest acknowledgment that someone I loved tried to destroy my life became the foundation for my healing.

The next stage involved establishing clear boundaries. Forgiveness doesn't mean allowing harmful people continued access to your life. I made the decision that while I could forgive my friend, I would never again allow them into my world. I began to understand that forgiveness and reconciliation do not go hand in hand. I could release my anger and resentment without having to talk to my friend ever again. I didn't need to confront them, I didn't need to yell at them, and I didn't need to even let them know that I knew they betrayed me.

This understanding didn't come all at once. It came in layers, like the German chocolate cake Michael taught me to make.

I started to see how holding on to anger at my friend's betrayal was actually keeping me tethered to the very system I wanted to be free from. My resentment had become another form of surveillance—self-surveillance, constant vigilance against future hurt. I slowly realized I could learn to live with the hard, painful truth that trust sometimes gets broken.

What surprised me was how this work physically changed me. I would sit and write letters to my friend, dumping my consciousness and energy onto the paper. I knew I would never send these letters, so I would burn them after, allowing the energy to transform into something else. With each releasing ritual, I could feel my body's chemistry shifting. The tightness in my chest around my heart would release. The tension in my jaw would subside. My sleep would deepen.

Years later, I'd learn about research showing how forgiveness reduces cortisol levels, our stress hormone, reducing inflammation in the body, and relaxing our physical body. When we hold on to anger and resentment, it causes constriction in the body as if we are physically closed off from the world in a stance of protective guarding. Forgiveness causes relaxation and relaxation is expansion. We also manifest more easily from a place of relaxation versus tension. Forgiveness is freedom, freedom to let go, freedom to create your next life without being attached to or closed down by the past. Forgiveness is peace.

Most importantly, I found that forgiveness isn't about the other person at all. It's about you. We're often taught that forgiveness is a two-way process: Someone apologizes, and in return, we forgive them.

But real forgiveness doesn't require anyone else's participation. It's a solo journey, one we commit to because we want to be free.

My friend never apologized. They never acknowledged what they'd done, never explained why they chose to betray years of friendship and trust. Before this event, I thought in order to forgive someone I'd need something from them, in the form of an explanation, an apology, or some sign of regret. I thought I needed closure through an exchange that let me know the other person felt sorry for the pain they caused me. Through this experience, I learned I could forgive and release myself from the pain.

Perhaps the most difficult part of my forgiveness was returning to the teachings I had learned in Kirtan and in Erich's classes: We are all one. We have no enemies. We are all universally connected. From this foundation, I started forming empathy for my friend and even understanding. I was able to put myself in their shoes and connect with their energy, seeing a part of myself in them. Once I was able to do this, I immediately understood why they had betrayed me and, on some level, it even made sense to me. They had chosen themselves and their family. They had chosen their freedom. They made what must have been a very difficult choice, and it wasn't in my favor. I learned to respect that, knowing that we all make choices for different reasons and some of the choices come at the expense of others' peace.

I didn't excuse their actions or minimize the impact they had on me. Rather, I acknowledged our shared humanness. I had to admit that while I would never betray someone as they had betrayed me, I too had made choices in my life that hurt others. This recognition helped me step back from the black-and-white thinking that kept me trapped in the pain of betrayal.

As Ram Dass says, "We are all just walking each other home." Everyone we meet in this world has a place and a purpose in our lives, as we do in theirs. Everyone on this planet is karmically connected, or we wouldn't exist together at this time. And everyone on our immediate path brings us into our evolution. Everyone holds a piece of the puzzle that walks us home to ourselves and our own form of enlightenment.

From this more openhearted perspective, I could see how even this betrayal was placed on my path for a reason. I began asking myself what this experience was teaching me about myself, about my patterns, about my own resilience. The experience took me to a deeper level of my understanding of human connectedness. When we open our hearts to others in the form of forgiveness, we open ourselves to the greater meaning of our lives. We remember that we have no enemies and that everyone walking this planet shares our energy. When we hurt someone, we hurt ourselves. When we refuse to forgive someone, we refuse to forgive ourselves. We are all connected.

True forgiveness is a form of release that opens our hearts in profound ways. And it's completely independent of the other person's actions or awareness. It's about releasing the grip that anger, betrayal, and resentment have on your own heart and energy. It takes precious resources to hold on to anger. When we spend time holding on to past resentment, we spend energy that could be used for manifesting the life we desire. In forgiving someone, we not only open our hearts to our universal connectedness, we also take back our energy and power to create the life we want.

True forgiveness is a choice, one we have to revisit repeatedly. I'd have moments when I thought I'd fully forgiven, only to have rage resurface when a particular memory arose. Each time, I had to consciously choose forgiveness again. Rather than being discouraged by this, I came to see these moments as opportunities to deepen my commitment to myself and to reclaim my power instead of giving it away to anger about the past.

I also came to understand that before I could fully forgive another, I needed to forgive myself. This turned out to be far more challenging than I anticipated. I was holding myself to an impossible standard—believing I should have somehow known better, seen the betrayal coming, protected myself from the pain. I spent weeks beating myself up for not noticing the red flags that now seem so apparent. The voice of self-judgment was relentless, and it took a tremendous commitment to listen to it and to eventually quiet it. Self-forgiveness required me to acknowledge that I had done the best I could with the awareness I had at the time. It meant treating myself with the same compassion I was finding for the friend who betrayed me. The breakthrough came when I realized the self-judgment was just another form of my old patterns of perfectionism—ones that were not serving me. I expected myself to know better, to make flawless choices. I blamed myself for not being perfect.

Eventually, I had to forgive myself for being human, for being imperfect, for making choices based on trust rather than suspicion and fear. I also had to trust that this betrayal was part of my life path and, in some ways, that my intuition and Higher Self had led me to it to learn. They had led me to every other circumstance on my path—why not this one too?

Forgiveness became my portal to freedom. When I stopped pouring energy into anger at my friend, at the situation, at myself for "getting into this mess," something transformed. That energy returned to me, available now for healing and growth. I began to see how even this betrayal had strengthened me, teaching me to trust my inner voice when it warned me to honor my boundaries, to navigate challenges with wisdom instead of fear. By forgiving, I declared that the past no longer controlled my present peace. The pain was my teacher, not my master.

The journey to forgiveness isn't easy. In fact, it's the hardest form of release we'll ever practice. But it's also the most transformative. Think about it: How much of your energy is currently tied up in old resentments? How many times do you replay past hurts, feeding them with your attention and life force? Each moment spent in anger about the past is a moment you're not fully present in your own life, not fully available to create your future.

What I didn't completely appreciate until I walked this path was that forgiveness requires grieving. I needed to mourn what was lost, including the friendship I thought I had and the trust that was broken. This grief is a necessary part of the forgiveness. By allowing myself to truly feel the sadness of what I had lost, I created space for something new to be born.

I invite you to ask yourself who you need to forgive to wholly claim your power—and this person could be yourself. You can find forgiveness. You can open your heart, grieve, and take your energy back from anger and resentment. You can choose to forgive not because what happened was okay, but because you deserve to be free. The ability to turn betrayal into growth and to choose freedom over resentment is part of your power.

Start small. Notice where you're holding on to old hurts. Maybe it's anger at a parent who didn't show up the way you needed. Maybe it's resentment toward an ex who betrayed your trust. Maybe it's regret for choices you wish you'd made differently. Each of these resentments is like a weight, using up precious energy that could be directed toward manifesting the life you deserve.

Forgiveness also doesn't require the other person's participation. You don't need their apology, their acknowledgment, or their change of behavior. You don't even need to maintain a relationship with them. Forgiveness is a gift you give yourself, the gift of energetic freedom and profound healing.

And yes, you can do this. The same strength that's gotten you through every challenge in your life, the same resilience that's helped you survive every storm. That's the strength that can help you forgive. It's not about doing it perfectly or all at once. It's about choosing, again and again, to release what no longer serves you.

When you find yourself struggling to forgive, remember that every bit of energy you spend holding on to past pain is energy you can't use to create what you want. Your power to manifest the life you desire becomes fully available only when you release what's holding you back.

This is your invitation to freedom. To take all that amazing energy you've been using to maintain your resentments and redirect it toward your dreams. To remember that forgiveness isn't about being perfect. It's about being free.

Chapter Fourteen
LEARNING TO TRUST LIFE AGAIN

After forgiving my friend's betrayal and finding sanctuary in Michael's house, I began to feel something stir within me, a tiny seed of possibility. Forgiveness had freed me from the burden of resentment, but it had also opened a more difficult question: Could I learn to trust again? Not just others, but life itself?

There's a particular kind of courage required to put down roots when you've grown accustomed to running. After years of living in survival mode—couch surfing, avoiding paper trails, staying off the grid—I found myself facing perhaps the scariest challenge yet: choosing to trust life again.

The decision to start rebuilding arrived in small moments that slowly accumulated into a different way of being. It began with a yoga studio owner asking if I'd consider teaching regular classes. The old me would have immediately declined, knowing that putting my name on a schedule meant being findable, traceable, vulnerable. But I was changing. Maybe it was exhaustion from years of hiding, or maybe it was my soul quietly insisting that it was time to live again. Whatever the reason, I heard myself say yes.

That first yes became a doorway to more. Within weeks, I found myself looking at apartments; real apartments, not temporary sublets or friends' spare rooms. I remember standing in what would become my first real home in years, sunlight streaming through the windows, the agent waiting expectantly with a lease agreement.

My hand trembled slightly as I signed my name, committing myself to twelve months in one place. It felt simultaneously terrifying and exhilarating. Something in me knew this was the place where I would rebuild my life. And I followed that knowing, even though it made me feel raw and exposed.

Then came a four-month-old rescue puppy. When I first saw her at the shelter, something in my heart cracked open. After years of guarding myself against attachment, avoiding anything that could make me vulnerable, here was this tiny being who needed me completely. The decision to adopt her wasn't just about getting a dog, it was about choosing to love again, choosing to let myself be needed.

I named her Juno, after the asteroid and goddess, a celestial guardian watching over my journey back to trust. Her dependence on me was terrifying at first. Each morning, as I filled her food bowl or took her for a walk, my mind would spiral into anxious questions: What if I wasn't here next week to take care of her? What if everything fell apart again? What if I couldn't be the person she needed me to be?

These fears weren't really about Juno. They were about my own wounded relationship with permanence, with commitment, with love itself. Each time she curled up in my lap or wagged her tail at my return, I had to face another layer of my own vulnerability. But something magical happened in those moments of fear: I discovered I could handle them. I could feel the terror of attachment and still choose to stay. And I found love was what happened when I chose to stay.

Through this journey with Juno, I began to develop a different relationship with my fear. Instead of seeing it as an enemy to be conquered or a weakness to be overcome, I started to recognize it as a part of myself, but not my whole self. I didn't have to get rid of it, I just needed to listen to it and then remember it was only a part of me, a part that had protected me for a long time. A part that deserved a place at the table of my mind, but it deserved only one spot and it could never be at the head of the table.

Years later, I would discover that what I was instinctively doing aligned with a therapeutic approach called internal family systems (IFS), a psychological framework that views the mind as containing multiple parts, each with its own perspective and job to do. But at the time, I just knew that fighting against my fear had never worked. It only made the fear shout louder. Listening to it and seeing it as part of myself helped put it at ease and helped me expand into a new person, one who felt whole, complete, and ready to live again.

What I came to understand was that my fear was a protective part of me that had been working overtime for years. In IFS terms, this would be called a "manager" part, a protector that had been trying to keep me safe by maintaining constant vigilance. This part had kept me alert when federal agents were watching, had guided me away from dangerous situations, had helped me survive years of uncertainty. It had earned its place in my inner council.

My meditation practice became the space where I learned to have conversations with this protective part. I would sit quietly and let it speak, really listening to what it had to say. Sometimes it would show up as a tightness in my chest, sometimes as a parade of worst-case scenarios marching through my mind. Instead of trying to silence these expressions, I would acknowledge them: "I hear you. I understand why you're worried. Thank you for trying to keep me safe."

What I didn't know then but would later learn through IFS was that I was doing something called "unblending," separating my core self from the protective part that was trying to run the show. By acknowledging the fear part without becoming completely identified with it, I was creating space for a relationship with it rather than being consumed by it.

This practice of sitting with my fear part, rather than fighting it or running from it, gradually changed my relationship with it. Fear was no longer the dictator of my decisions but rather an advisor, sometimes a rather dramatic one, but an advisor nonetheless. When I considered signing the lease on my apartment, my fear part showed up right on schedule with its list of concerns. But now, instead of letting this part derail me, I could say, "I hear you. Yes, this is risky. Yes, this makes us vulnerable. And I'm choosing to do it anyway."

I wasn't rejecting my fear part or trying to get rid of it; I was acknowledging its protective intention while gently taking the lead on decisions that aligned with who my core self really was and wanted to become. The truth of who I was and had always been started to shine through the fear, and the more I leaned into that light the more fear subsided.

As I settled into this new relationship with my fear part, something subtle but powerful began to shift in my inner landscape. Just as I had learned to listen to this part of myself during those years of survival, letting it guide me away from danger and keep me safe, I now began to recognize another voice growing stronger: my intuition. It wasn't that fear disappeared completely; rather, it ceased to be the loudest voice in the room.

My intuition was free to take center stage. It had always been with me, but it sometimes took a backseat to fear. During those years of hiding and running, my fear part was a powerful player, attempting to drown out almost everything else. It had to be that way for a while; that hypervigilance had helped me survive and figure out what felt safe. But now, as the immediate dangers receded, I could begin to distinguish between my protective part's urgent warnings and my intuition's deeper knowing.

The difference was subtle but distinct. My fear part always shouted, always pushed, always constricted. It spoke in "what ifs" and worst-case scenarios. My intuition, on the other hand, came as a quiet certainty, a gentle knowing that expanded rather than contracted. Fear lived in my chest, tight and anxious. Intuition lived in my belly, solid and grounded.

I noticed how differently these aspects of my inner system guided me. My fear part had always been about avoid, repeating phrases like *don't go here, don't do that, don't trust anyone*. My intuition was about moving toward—go here, explore this, connect with that person. Fear focused on survival; intuition coaxed me toward thriving.

Just as I had honored my fear part's protective intentions during the dangerous times, I now learned to honor intuition's expansive guidance. When an opportunity to teach more yoga classes arose, my fear part predictably chimed in with its concerns about visibility and vulnerability. But underneath those familiar warnings, I could feel my intuition as it spoke: This is your path. Take it.

With this growing trust in my intuition, I felt ready to take another step toward reclaiming my life. Moving into my own apartment also meant I could finally unpack the boxes that had been in storage for nearly four years, since that frantic packing session right after Chad's initial arrest. When I opened the first one, I was hit with the memory of federal agents rifling through everything, how they'd left my belongings in disarray and my life scattered. Now I was the one putting things back in order, on my own terms. Each box was like a time capsule, holding pieces of my former life that had been waiting patiently to be rediscovered.

The first box I opened contained my crystals, which once sat with me while I learned to meditate and hold space for my intuition all those years ago. Holding them again after so many years, I could feel their powerful energy in my palms, reminding me of who I used to be, the student of energy and consciousness. They were a bridge between my past and present selves.

Then came the books, boxes and boxes of them. Each one felt like greeting an old friend. There was *Prometheus Rising*, which I had been halfway through when everything fell apart. I found my old astrology books, their pages filled with handwritten natal charts and notes about everything I knew and wanted to know about the stars. Seeing my own handwriting from years ago was strangely moving, evidence of a time when I had the luxury of studying everything and anything that called my attention.

As I unpacked the boxes and arranged my astrology books on the shelves, my new roommate, Stella, became curious. "You know astrology?" she asked, eyeing the collection. When she asked me to draw her natal chart, something deep within me woke up and remembered how as a teenager I had lived my life by the cosmos.

I spent hours with Stella, explaining her placements, the aspects between planets, the story the stars were telling about her soul's journey. As I spoke, I could feel myself coming alive in a way I hadn't in years. The language of the cosmos flowed through me as if it had just been waiting for permission to emerge again. In those hours of sharing this ancient wisdom with Stella, I remembered a piece of myself that I had almost forgotten.

This reconnection with astrology sparked something larger. I began following the moon phases again, finding comfort in their monthly rhythms that had nothing to do with court dates or legal concerns. After years of keeping my focus narrow, watching for threats, staying alert for danger, I could finally lift my eyes to the skies again. I could look up without the fear of tripping over something.

The moon's journey through its phases reminded me that life moves in cycles, that darkness always gives way to light, that nothing—not even fear—lasts forever. I began writing down the moon phase and placement every day in my journal, asking myself how the energy was making me feel in that moment and how I could use it to guide my day. I had no idea at the time, but this would become the foundation of my work as Spirit Daughter.

I began to live by the lunar cycles. I was practicing Ashtanga yoga at the time. In Ashtanga yoga, you practice the same set of poses in order each day. I practiced every day at 6 a.m. except Saturdays and except new or full moon days. The theory in Ashtanga is that one does not have enough energy to practice on a new moon and has too much energy to practice on a full moon. Either too much or too little energy (because of overconfidence) could lead to injury.

I found myself up at 6 a.m. every new or full moon day with nothing to do. I began my own practice on new and full moon days. I went to the twenty-four-hour Korean spa downtown, where I could restore on new moons as I journaled about the energy, and I could dip in the many pools to release energy that no longer served me on the full moon.

These moon rituals gave me something I desperately needed: a framework for understanding change. After years of unpredictable chaos, there was a powerful comfort in the reliable waxing and waning of the moon. I could look up at the night sky and know exactly where in its cycle the moon was. I could trust its movement regardless of what was happening in my life. The moon became my constant companion, a cosmic reminder that even when everything else felt uncertain, some rhythms remained the same.

With each passing month of moon ritual, I found myself exhaling fears I hadn't even realized I was holding. The persistent background anxiety, that hypervigilance that had kept me scanning for threats, began to lose its grip. At the Korean spa during full moons, as I submerged myself in the healing waters, I would consciously release specific fears. I let go of the fear of being found, the fear of my life collapsing again, the fear of trusting and being hurt. I would visualize these fears dissolving into the water, being carried away far from me.

But there was still one fear I needed to face: the possibility of a sealed indictment with my name on it. A sealed indictment was an invisible threat hanging over my head; it would mean charges had been filed against me but were being kept secret from public view. Even my lawyer couldn't look it up to confirm or deny its existence. The not knowing was excruciating and kept me from fully living my life. I had to face it head-on.

This fear had kept me bound within invisible walls for years. I wouldn't travel, wouldn't venture too far from my safe spaces, always half expecting federal agents to appear. But as I developed this new relationship with my fear parts, I began to see how this particular fear was actually offering me a path to release. If there really was a sealed indictment, the surest way to find out would be to try to leave the country. They wouldn't let someone under federal indictment just hop on an international flight.

As I prepared for that first flight to Cabo, Jake, the same friend I first spilled the beans to in the car ride back from the desert, offered me a spiritual tool that would become a constant through all my future travels: the Ganesha mantra. *Om Gam Ganapataye Namaha.* Ganesha, the elephant-headed deity in Hindu tradition, is known as the remover of obstacles and the guardian of new beginnings. *Om*—the primordial sound of the Universe, reminding me that I was part of something vast and eternal. *Gam*—the seed sound that awakens Ganesha's energy, helping me clear the path ahead. *Ganapataye*, lord of all beings, teaching me that every experience, even the painful ones, served a higher purpose. *Namaha*, I bow to this wisdom, I surrender to this journey. I recited this mantra like my life depended on it as I walked through security. It was my lifeline through a very anxiety-producing trip and my connection to something larger than my fear.

The moment my feet touched Mexican soil, I felt lightness take over my body. I had made it to Cabo in one piece, and more importantly, I had crossed an international border without being detained. The relief was immediate, another weight lifting from my shoulders.

For the first time in years, I felt true freedom. I ran down the beach barefoot, feeling the warm sand between my toes, laughing at the pure joy of movement. I jumped on a boat with people I'd just met, something the hypervigilant me would never have done. I even posted for the first time on my personal Instagram account, a digital footprint I'd been avoiding for years.

The defining moment came during a boat ride to an offshore island. As we cut through the turquoise water, the coastline of Cabo fading behind us, I felt as though I could keep going forever. All my fear, all my heartache seemed to belong to another lifetime, another person. As I inhaled the smell of the salt water, I felt a different part of me take over, my core essence, the part that felt clear and calm. The part that knew with absolute certainty that everything was going to be okay.

Something within me healed on that trip. Something deeper than my heartbreak, deeper than my fear. Standing on foreign soil, passport stamped, I realized I could have a life. I could be free. I could look past the next month and actually start to envision a future. On the next new moon after that trip, I wrote down my first vision for my life. It wasn't anything elaborate. I simply saw myself living in Venice Beach in one of the California bungalows this area is known for. It had a white fence and beautiful flowers around it. The best part was that I owned this home. It couldn't be taken from me. I couldn't be kicked out. And once I had that vision, I could hear the faint laughter of children in the yard. I could finally feel something other than fear. I could feel a life that felt, for lack of a better word, "normal."

I also knew that I wanted to travel more. I wanted to feel freedom through exploring the world. I had been in California for years; it was time to get out and experience something else. I was a yoga teacher without a ton of commitments other than my dog, Juno. Now was the time to wander.

Each new destination became a doorway to another piece of myself. In Peru, I found myself climbing Machu Picchu with a group of strangers who would teach me something powerful about resilience and community. As we ascended the ancient steps, each one steeper than the last, I felt my own strength building, not just physically, but spiritually. My body ached, an extreme discomfort that forced me into complete presence. I couldn't think about the past or worry about the future; all that existed was the next step, the next breath. In this pure physical meditation, all I could feel was the beautiful moment in front of me.

At one particularly challenging point, when the altitude made every breath feel strained, someone in our group started singing "We Are the Champions." Soon we were all belting it out, our voices unifying in the energy of strength. In that moment, each step up that mountain wasn't just about reaching the summit, it was about healing an old story and writing a new one.

When we finally reached the top, fog had settled over the ancient citadel, wrapping the stone structures in what felt like a magical mist.

While other tourists busied themselves taking photos, I found a quiet spot away from the crowds and sat in meditation. I could feel the energy of this sacred place. There was a heightened frequency here that seemed to vibrate through the stones themselves. I opened myself to it completely, feeling the ancient wisdom held in this location flow through me.

As I sat overlooking the valley below, I reconnected with the part of myself that felt calm, clear, and ready to face whatever came next. I felt connected to the Universe, to eons of knowledge, and to the power held in this location where countless others had come seeking wisdom before me.

Later that night, lying under a blanket of stars so bright and numerous they seemed close enough to touch, I had a revelation. This whole journey, not just the mountain climb, but every step of my life path, had been chosen by my soul for its evolution. From the moment I was born, my energy had selected these exact lessons, even the hardest ones, for my growth.

The Universe was cocreating with me in my own transformation. And I was the champion of all the experiences I had chosen so far. I was beginning to see my challenges from a different perspective, not as bad choices, but as the very struggle that was teaching me to evolve in a way I would have never imagined all those years ago when I had first left graduate school. I had met each challenge in front of me. And while I still hadn't totally taken my power back to design my life as I wanted, I was close. I could feel it.

After Peru, I headed to Spain and France. In France, I found another layer of healing in an eleventh-century chapel in Bordeaux. As I walked down the aisle between rows of worn wooden pews, I gazed up at the centuries-old stained-glass windows. Colored light streamed through them, mesmerizing my heart and holding it.

Standing in that ancient space, surrounded by centuries of prayers and revelations, another old shell cracked inside me. Perhaps it was the beauty that finally opened my heart fully, or maybe it was the sense of safety I felt in this sacred space. Whatever the catalyst, I found myself sobbing uncontrollably, but these weren't tears of sadness. The chapel's energy seemed to hold me and my pain, helping me find gratitude for my journey. It helped me develop a compassion for myself I'd never experienced before.

There, beneath vaulted ceilings, I could finally see my experience with Chad for what it was: a beautiful tragedy. The love we shared, the connection we had, even the pain of its ending. It was all beautifully tragic. Understanding the journey from this perspective helped me find gratitude for it and understand that it, like everything else, unfolded exactly as it needed to. I learned so much from that relationship and I wouldn't change any of it. It made me who I am today, and I love that person. In that beautiful chapel in Bordeaux, I realized that I loved who I had become and without my story I wouldn't be her. And even though I hadn't been in a formal church or chapel since I was a kid, and nor would I return after, I believe I found this particular chapel on yet another sacred energy location of the world because my soul and intuition led me there. It felt connected to the energy center I felt at the top of Machu Picchu and healed me in the same way.

Inhaling the faint scent of incense, I finally understood that even if I could, I wouldn't change any piece of my journey, not even the hardest parts. They had shaped me into who I was and who I could become. I could feel the next version of myself starting to take shape and I was so excited to meet her. I also felt an immense gratitude for all the women I'd been. These versions of myself carried me to the other side of a long journey, and in that moment, my heart felt connected to all of them.

After that trip, I no longer feared heartbreak; I saw it as a beautiful part of my story. I was grateful to have loved so deeply, even though it ended. My heart cracked open in a way that showed me I would love again. Perhaps someone else with that same intensity, but first and most importantly, myself. I could finally forgive every choice I'd made on my path because those choices had shaped me into exactly who I was meant to be.

There, of course, were moments I felt my old heartache. There were also moments of fear. I countered them with gratitude for my life. I found solace in the "*ands*." I was still grieving a former love *and* I was building a magical life. Some days I still woke up with a heavy heart *and* I loved my new apartment. I made some serious mistakes in my past *and* I had the wisdom to turn them into lessons. If I had replaced any "*ands*" with "*buts*" I would have lost something. I would have negated the previous sentiment and not felt the whole truth of my life. Living the whole truth, though, is where I found the most magic, power, and inner knowing.

Each destination I traveled to over that year transformed my relationship with myself in distinct ways. Cabo helped me feel truly free, breaking through the invisible walls I'd built around myself. Machu Picchu connected me to something far beyond myself, reminding me that I was more powerful than my fears and I could climb any physical, mental, or emotional mountain in front of me. And Bordeaux gave me a new compassion and understanding for my journey, allowing me to see even heartbreak as something to be grateful to have experienced.

The mantra that had carried me through airport security took on new meaning with each journey. With each destination, my fear part relaxed its grip a little more. It was still present. It was still offering its protective wisdom when needed, but it was no longer in charge of my decisions. Each passport stamp, each new adventure, each moment of beauty and connection became evidence that I could trust life again. My fear part began to understand that the world beyond my carefully constructed safety zone wasn't just survivable—it was amazing, and so was I.

I also began to see that some obstacles were actually doorways, that some wounds were actually portals to wisdom, and that some endings were actually beautiful beginnings in disguise. Learning to trust life again wasn't about waiting for everything to feel safe, it was about discovering that I could handle whatever came my way, that every step of my journey, even the hardest ones, was leading me home to myself.

If you're reading these words, there's likely some fear holding you back from the life you most desire to live. Maybe it's not a sealed indictment or federal agents, but maybe it's the fear of leaving a secure job to follow your passion, the fear of opening your heart after heartbreak, or the fear of being seen for who you truly are. Whatever form it takes, fear has a way of making us feel small, of convincing us to live within the confines of what feels safe rather than expanding into the full possibility of our lives.

I believe, though, that you can face the fears that have been holding you back. You can learn to work with them rather than being paralyzed by them. Just as I discovered that fear could be an advisor rather than a dictator, you too can develop a new relationship with your fears.

Start where you are. You don't have to climb Machu Picchu or move across the country tomorrow. Begin by simply acknowledging your fears without trying to silence them. Listen to what they're trying to tell you. There's often wisdom hidden within their warnings. Thank them for trying to protect you, and then gently remind them that you're stronger than they think you are.

Remember that awakening to your fear is the first step toward freedom from it. When you can name what's holding you back, when you can feel where it lives in your body, when you can recognize its voice in your mind, that's when you begin to have a choice about how to respond to it. That's when you can start choosing your life beyond fear.

You are amazing. Your fear wants you to forget this truth, but I'm here to remind you: You are made of the same energy as stars. You have within you the power to transform any fear into fuel for your evolution. And even if you don't believe in yourself, I believe in you. And I know someday you'll believe in yourself too.

The path from fear to trust isn't always straight, and it isn't always smooth. There will be days when fear feels overwhelming, when trust feels out of reach, when every step forward feels like walking through mud. That's okay. That's part of the journey. What matters isn't that you never feel afraid. What matters is that you don't let fear have the final say in your story.

Trust builds through action. Each time you take a step forward despite your fear, you're building evidence that you can trust yourself. You can trust your intuition. You can believe in yourself to overcome fear and expand into a new reality, one aligned with your highest visions.

So, take that first step. Have that conversation you've been avoiding. Apply for that dream job. Open your heart to that possibility. Sign up for that class. Book that ticket. Whatever your version of facing fear looks like, know that you have everything you need within you to handle it. Know that on the other side of that fear is a version of yourself and your life that's more beautiful than you can imagine.

Chapter Fifteen
YOU ARE THE LIGHT

After traveling the world and rediscovering my freedom, I found myself at another crossroads, one that felt more significant than any I'd faced before. My passport was stamped with evidence that I could move freely across borders, that no sealed indictment was waiting to trap me, that life could expand beyond the confines of my fears. The trips to Cabo, Peru, and France had served as progressive tests of my newfound freedom. Each journey stretched my comfort zone a little further, each return confirmed that I truly could come and go anywhere without consequence.

But as I settled back into my Venice apartment, Juno greeting me with her boundless enthusiasm after each trip, a deeper question began to surface—one that couldn't be answered by simply booking another flight. The adventures had proven I could survive outside my fear and could navigate foreign streets while exhaling. But could I dare to dream?

The question now pressing on me was: Could I actually build a life?

Not a temporary shelter of moment-to-moment existence, but a stable, intentional life where I could live the dreams I had suppressed for years? Could I move beyond "In this moment, I am okay" to "In this life, I am free to choose"?

The hardest part about dreaming isn't the dreaming itself. It's believing you have the right to dream at all. After years of living moment to moment, breath to breath, the very idea of looking beyond the present felt not just impossible, but almost dangerous. Like tempting fate. Like asking for disappointment. Like setting myself up for another heartbreak.

I had become so good at surviving the present moment that I'd forgotten there was anything else. My world had shrunk to the size of my next breath, my next step, my next action. It was safe there, in that tiny space of now. But safety, I was beginning to understand, could become its own kind of prison.

Elena Brower came into my life through another yoga mentor, arriving exactly when I needed her guidance most. She was an esteemed yoga practitioner whose presence commanded respect not through force but through her grounded wisdom and a deep connection to ancient teachings. When she agreed to consult with me, it felt like the Universe opening another door.

Our conversations happened in the wee early morning hours, me in California fresh from my run with Juno, her in New York already deep into her day. What struck me most about Elena was that she never asked for my story. She didn't need to know where I'd been to help me see where I could go. She simply made it her mission to help me move forward, to plant seeds of possibility I didn't even know existed.

I remember one morning clearly. I was still sweating from my sunrise run, my breath coming in quick puffs as I answered her call.

"It's time," she said, her voice carrying that quiet certainty I'd come to trust, "to dissolve your commitments to the past and make space for new commitments to your future."

I felt my body tense, that familiar contraction of fear. "I don't know if I can," I admitted. "What if—"

"What if what?" she interrupted. "What if everything falls apart? What if you get hurt? What if you fail?" She paused, letting those questions hang in the air. "But what if you get everything you ask for?"

The very idea that I could create any life I wanted was a radical concept for me. I hadn't even allowed myself to think about next year, let alone my entire life. What was I going to do with an entire life? But if I was going to figure it out, I needed to follow her advice and fully release my commitments to my past. My past pain, my past regret, my past love, my past fear. It all needed to go. No more letting yesterday dictate tomorrow. I was ready to dream of a real future, one spacious enough to hold every possibility starting to stir within me.

That conversation became a turning point. I began to understand that the present would always be my home, but I could venture out from it to shape my future. Living in the moment had saved me during the chaos, and it would remain my foundation. Now I was learning I could stand firmly in today while also envisioning a life beyond this moment. The present wasn't a hiding place anymore. It was my launching pad.

Elena suggested I start writing intentions. Not goals or plans. Those felt too concrete, too demanding, too easy to fail at. Intentions were different. They were like planting seeds. You could nurture them without knowing exactly what they would grow into. They were an exercise in possibility rather than certainty.

Just as I had written that first vision on the new moon about my house in Venice, I could start to see how this practice done regularly could heal me. I used the lunar energy to help me write more visions under Elena's guidance. At first, my intentions were small, almost apologetic. I wrote them like someone testing the temperature of the ocean—with one toe instead of diving into the first large wave. What I didn't realize was that these simple intentions were becoming the foundation of my entire life, creating containers for new energy to unfold within and around me.

I was still a step away from fully understanding the power I held to manifest my life through these intentions. But even in their simplest form, they were planting seeds that would shift how I moved through each day. This, I would later learn, is where all transformation begins—with feeling. We must feel the change in our bodies before we can envision it in our minds or create it in our lives.

My background in neuroscience, though I'd left that career path years ago, gave me a unique perspective on what was happening in my brain during this transition. The research on manifestation, intention-setting, and neural plasticity had always fascinated me, and now I was living it firsthand.

What I was experiencing had a neurological explanation, one that validated the power of intention and visualization rather than dismissing it as wishful thinking. For years, my brain in its hypervigilant state had suppressed my ability to create big visions for my future. I was in a constant state of fight-or-flight. In order to start dreaming I needed to relax and activate my parasympathetic nervous system—the part of the body involved in resting and digesting. This is the system we need to set intentions and manifest them, not the hypervigilant sympathetic nervous system that gets activated when we are in fear.

Our fight-or-flight response evolved eons ago and served us well throughout human evolution. It's outdated for our current times, though. We treat everyday stresses like our very life is in danger even if it's just a harsh email from our boss. We are walking around with a system designed for a different part of human history. My sympathetic nervous system had been on overdrive for years and that constant activation took its toll on my ability to dream. My brain had literally become wired for hypervigilance and survival.

Through meditation and yoga, I was slowly moving into a state of relaxation. Not one that was temporary, but one that was becoming my default way of being. I would wake up surprised that my breathing was deep. I no longer felt like a raw nerve with most of the world feeling hard to bear. Through conscious practice, I was slowly moving from fight-or-flight into relax and digest. This state, I would learn, is the foundation for manifestation.

Remember when I told you about that fascinating filter on your brain called the reticular activating system (RAS)? You know, the one I basically blew the lid off when I had a mental breakdown/kundalini awakening. Well, that filter changes its criteria depending on your level of perceived stress. If you're in a state of fight-or-flight, that filter narrows and allows in less information. When your nervous system is downregulated—that is, relaxed—it allows in more. Makes sense. If you're being hunted down by a wild boar, you'd only want to focus on information pertaining to that, not the birds chirping or some amazing discovery around the next bend.

The best part about the RAS? You can program it. And while you have the ability to program your RAS no matter the state of your nervous system, you have much more flexibility and wider parameters when you are in a downregulated state. And in my opinion, you're a much more intentional programmer when you're relaxed and not stressed out. You also have a greater capacity to hear your intuition and use that wisdom to help you direct your attention and your RAS. And what does intention-setting do? You guessed it, it programs this magical filter to let in information that supports the manifestation of your intentions.

If you were to set intentions around finding a new job, you are essentially programming your RAS to allow information into your brain about opportunities that could lead to this new job. Information that might have otherwise been filtered out. Because remember, we're filtering out most of the world around us. Most of it never makes its way to our conscious mind. But when we set intentions, we adjust the filter. When we're relaxed, we can create more flexible, expansive filters that look for opportunities not threats. We can focus on best-case scenarios not worst-case ones. We'll then find evidence of those best-case scenarios and the information we need to actively create them in our lives. This is where signs and serendipity come in. We see the sign because we've told our brain to find it. And our brains do what we tell them to do.

Now because I'm me, I'll take this one step further. On a new moon, I believe we have greater access to our intuition, our real desires, and are more prone to nervous system downregulation. This last bit is why the Ashtanga yogis don't like to practice on a new moon, because we don't have enough energy to complete the rigorous sequence. We are in a perfect state, though, for parasympathetic activation through meditation, relaxation, and simply doing nothing.

On a new moon, we're more receptive and so is our brain. We can access our intuition to inform our intentions, making them more powerful to our entire energy. We can actually feel them and get lost in visualizing them, training our brain to accept them when they start manifesting. Here's another part of manifestation we don't always talk about: Your brain will naturally resist anything you're trying to manifest that is outside of its comfort zone. Your brain likes the familiar even if it's not your dream. It will do anything to stay in its familiar territory, including sabotaging your best efforts to manifest the next version of yourself.

When you set intentions, visualize, and feel them, you activate areas of the brain that would be involved if these intentions were real. You are telling your brain they are already happening and they are safe. When you begin actually manifesting your intentions in reality, your brain accepts them. It doesn't block them because they already feel familiar. Intention-setting is literally programming your brain.

Intention-setting became my most powerful tool for transformation. By repeatedly focusing my attention on specific intentions while in a downregulated state, I essentially rewired my brain from being in a constant state of fear, subconsciously scanning the environment for threats, to a relaxed playground where new opportunities and futures were allowed in. I began consciously, and even subconsciously, programming my brain to seek out experiences that made me feel the way I wanted to feel.

Gradually, with Elena's gentle encouragement, my intentions began to grow beyond words on paper. They became programs for a new way of being, bridges between who I was and who I could become. I started to dream not just about surviving, but about thriving. Not just about getting through the day without an anxiety attack, but about creating something meaningful.

During this time, I also began what would become a lifelong practice. Each morning at 5:30 a.m., before my meditation, I would start by opening myself to receiving. The words were simple but powerful: "I am open to receiving love and beauty. I am open to receiving my intuition. I am open to receiving my path."

This practice wasn't complex or overly complicated. Just me sitting there in the hours before dawn, inviting in the energy I needed and wanted in my life. Over the years, the specific words have shifted and evolved, but the practice remains constant. Even now, I begin each day with this ritual of opening, this simple acknowledgment that I am ready to receive whatever wisdom, whatever guidance, whatever magic the Universe has to offer.

What I didn't realize then was that these morning declarations were doing more than just starting my day. They were gradually rewiring my relationship with possibility. Each morning, I was choosing to be open, receptive, and willing to receive what I needed. Instead of living in a closed-down, protective energetic stance, I opened, and this opening was my energy and consciousness's way of practicing trust in its most basic form.

Anxiety, I realized, always came with a contraction. It made my world smaller, my breathing shallower, my possibilities fewer. It brought in self-doubt with its small moments of "what if everything goes wrong?" and showed me all the ways I could fail. From a neurological perspective, anxiety activates the brain's fight-or-flight response system, flooding our bodies with stress hormones and narrowing our conscious mind to focus only on potential dangers.

Intuition, on the other hand, felt like expansion. It opened doors rather than closing them. It came with a sense of lightness, of possibility, of "what if everything goes right?" Even when it was guiding me away from something, it felt like being led toward something better rather than running from something worse.

Learning to distinguish between these two voices became my daily practice. When an idea or possibility arose, I would check in with my body. Was I contracting or expanding? Was my breath getting shorter or deeper? Was my world getting smaller or larger? This simple practice became my compass as I began to dream again.

I learned very quickly that it was nearly impossible to write intentions and even more impossible to manifest them from a state of anxiety. Manifestation doesn't work that way. We need to be open and receptive for our nervous system to relax enough to create a new reality or at least look for opportunities to build one.

Every time I wrote intentions, I first meditated, did some deep breathing, even lay on the ground to connect with the earth. These practices helped take me out of an anxious state and into an expansive one where I could plant real seeds for a future.

I also started writing affirmations. Every day, I would take pen to paper and write first a gratitude list, and second bold declarations of who I was becoming. I would write them in "I am" statements. And I would also write them in the form of "I believe I can create x, y, or z." I found that putting the statement "I believe I can" helped me believe in the possibility of creating a new life. Somewhere along the way I had lost this belief in myself. I had forgotten about my amazing power to create my life. These simple morning practices of opening, affirming, and writing intentions helped pave the way for a new future. One that felt like home.

I also found that dreaming again after being in survival mode is not just about imagining a better future. It's about believing you deserve that future. It's about healing the part of you that got so good at surviving that it forgot to look outside the box of now and see the future of what could be. It's about trusting not only your ability to create and manifest your dreams, but also your right to have them in the first place.

This was the real work—not just writing intentions, but believing in them. Not just imagining possibilities, but allowing myself to see a future beyond where I currently was in an apartment by the beach in Venice with my dog.

Taking action toward those dreams was even more challenging. I started small and let my intuition lead me. Instead of trying to plan my entire future, I would ask my intuition about just the next step. Should I take that yoga training? Should I write that blog post? Should I have coffee with that person who might become a friend? If it felt good to me, then I would do it. Sometimes I would even imagine the scenario and if I felt light in the vision, that would be an indicator that this was a good choice.

As I started believing in myself through affirmations and intentions, serendipity began to appear, those magical coincidences that feel like the Universe confirming you're on the right path. I know now that it wasn't just dumb luck; I was getting really good at programming my brain to find them. I would need something, and it would appear. I would have a question, and the answer would show up in an unexpected conversation or even a Facebook post.

I could have brushed off these coincidences as random events, but I didn't. I took them as signs from myself, from the Universe, from life itself that I was aligning with my soul's path and that I was on the right track to a life that I was meant to live. I was getting so clear on my visions that I could start to feel them materializing in front of me, and every sign I received made me believe in my power to create my life. And it felt like the Universe started believing that I would get it together and create the life I was intended to live.

During this time, I was in the space of "in-between." I wasn't quite my new self yet, but my old self was slowly dissolving. She was melting away, and as I stood there thanking her for helping me survive, I could feel my new self being formed. I had to honor this space, though. It didn't contain answers or five-year plans. It was flexible. It shifted, and I shifted with it. I experimented with new dreams, tried them on and asked how they felt. I let my mind wander, then I would rein it back in before it became destructive. I would ask for a sign if I needed it, knowing I would find it.

Life still felt unstable. I was shifting and changing into someone else, and I didn't quite know who that person was yet. I felt different and there was something scary about my new normal. I was standing on a bridge between who I had been and who I was becoming and it took a lot of courage to trust that bridge wouldn't collapse from underneath me. Something in me knew, though, that I had to keep trusting, keep moving forward, and keep committing to believing in myself. And so I did. I got up every day and committed to myself and my future, a future I could barely see but knew was waiting for me.

My intuition knew who I was before I did, and trusting it helped awaken me to my true purpose in life. Part of my journey was to go through heartache and fear, and find my power, all so that I could then turn that power toward helping others. I realized during this time that what I was going through wasn't about me, but about the journey I was born to live, and so I walked it gently, not knowing where I would land next. I had to trust that it would all work out some way and somehow.

I couldn't have known then that all of this would lead to the creation of Spirit Daughter, to helping others transform their lives through the very wisdom I was gaining through my own struggles. I couldn't have imagined that my journey through darkness would become a light for others finding their way. But my intuition knew. It had always known.

This is what I mean when I talk about trusting your path. It's not about understanding everything that happens to you. It's not about everything making sense in the moment. It's about trusting that your intuition is connected to something far more expansive and powerful than your logical mind can comprehend. It's about understanding that your intuition will lead you to some of your hardest truths so that you find your path.

Because that's what finding the light really means. It's not about it always being there. It's about remembering that you are the light. You always have been. Sometimes life brings us darkness. That's when we need to look for the light and become it. More importantly, we need to believe that we can be that light for ourselves and maybe even for others.

Your intuition is already speaking to you. Your dreams are already trying to find you. Your future is already reaching back to guide you forward. The real questions are: Are you ready to listen? Are you ready to dream? Are you ready to believe that you deserve every bit of magic you can imagine and probably more than you can imagine?

This is your invitation to expand beyond survival. To release your commitment to playing small or any other commitment that holds you back from your true brilliance. To trust that the same intuition that got you through your darkest moments can now lead you toward your brightest possibilities.

You don't have to see the whole path. You don't have to know how it will all work out. You just have to be willing to live in the space in between your old self and your new one. The rest will unfold as you go, just as it did for me.

Remember: Anxiety contracts, intuition expands. Fear makes your world smaller, trust makes it larger. The past may have taught you to survive, but the future is inviting you into a different vibration. One that is expansive and feels aligned with who you are meant to be. You get to choose which voice you listen to. You get to choose which path you follow. You get to choose whether to stay safe in the known or expand into the possible.

Choose expansion. Choose trust. Choose dreaming. Choose you.

Chapter Sixteen
WELCOME HOME

Every healing journey is one that involves a few steps forward followed by a few back. That's the nature of it; we need to revisit things from a new perspective to heal them from different angles until we finally find closure—sometimes when we least expect it.

It was August 2015. I began waking up at 4 a.m., unable to fall back asleep, every day. I've never been one to fight with my body, so when it wakes up, I get up. I've spent countless full moons journaling at 3 a.m. with a cup of tea and Juno by my side. I've practiced releasing rituals at 5 a.m. because my body and energy told me that was the best time. This sudden awakening at 4 a.m., though, was brought on by my heart. It needed to be held in the darkest hours before dawn. So, I gave my heart the attention it needed and deserved.

Each morning, I would fill my bathtub, creating a ritual of self-care in the morning hours before the world began and the business of life took over. These baths became releasing rituals. They were ceremonies of remembering who I was beneath all the layers of pain and protection I'd accumulated.

As I lowered myself into the water each morning, tears would come. Tears for my past pain. Tears for everything I had put myself through. Tears of remembering. Tears that let me know I was finally coming home to myself. I was mourning the person I used to be, honoring her and what she had guided me through, while releasing her. It felt like I was entering a new vibration of existence, one that could hold my future self. But first, before I could completely shift, I needed to revisit my old self one last time to say goodbye.

I created a sacred container to help me. Every morning I would thank the person I was, I would thank my old energy, and then I would declare that I was ready to release it. With each declaration, I would dunk my head under the water, feeling the releasing power of water. Then I would cry some more, letting the tears cleanse me.

Every day after I got out of the tub, I could feel another layer of old energy dissolving, transforming into something new. The water helped me alchemize my pain, not only releasing it but helping me to see the power in my pain, the story that would eventually help me inspire others through their pain.

It was during one of these morning rituals that I realized Venus was in retrograde in Leo, exactly where my natal Venus sits in my birth chart. I had studied birth charts and lunar phases for years now. Venus rules the heart and when in retrograde causes us to reflect on past pain. If the heart needs closure, it will often seek it during Venus retrograde. My heart took the cosmic opportunity to speak to me and ask me to heal the deepest part of it.

I had to confront the painful truth that I didn't feel worthy of the life I wanted to create. Growing up, I had been taught that worthiness was earned through achievements—good grades, prestigious degrees, societal approval. By those standards, I had completely messed up my life. A failed marriage, federal investigations, couch surfing. These weren't exactly the hallmarks of success.

But beneath this unworthiness lay something deeper: shame. Not just the fleeting embarrassment of making mistakes, but deep shame that made me question my very right to try again. It even made me question my right to have dreams in the first place. Who was I to think I could have an amazing life?

Shame eats away at our sense of possibility, our belief in our own resilience, and our connection to our amazingness. While unworthiness tells you you're not good enough, shame tells you you're flawed and don't deserve to even try to create something better.

From my neuroscience background, I understood that shame activates the brain differently than nearly any other emotion. What makes shame particularly destructive is how it affects our sense of self. Unlike guilt, which is about our behavior, shame takes over our identity. Shame had taken over my identity and was undermining my greatest efforts to create the life I wanted to live.

I discovered how shame had kept me confined and limited. It trapped me in patterns of self-doubt and hesitation. I found myself avoiding decisions, holding myself back, and refusing to step fully into my power. My conscious mind wanted these things, but my subconscious mind believed I didn't deserve them. Somewhere underneath my affirmations and intentions was a mantra that told me I was a failure.

Breaking free from shame's grip took a lot of work and self-compassion. I knew it was a road I had to walk if I was ever going to fully heal and take back my life. I realized I had to own my story completely. Not just the parts I could bear to look at and speak to others, but all of it—every choice, every mistake, every piece of it that made me feel like a failure.

I had to acknowledge that I had chosen all of it *and* I was still worthy of love despite my choices. Those choices might not have been perfect, but they were mine. And if I had the power to choose that life, I also had the power to choose something different.

I had to look directly at my shame and say, "Yes, I made those choices. Yes, some of them had painful consequences. And yes, I can still create something beautiful from here." I had to understand and believe that my ability to manifest the life I wanted to create wasn't dependent on my past being perfect.

During this time I was led to the research of Brené Brown, whose book *The Gifts of Imperfection* helped guide me out of this dark time brought on by Venus retrograde. Brown states that "Shame is that warm feeling that washes over us, making us feel small, flawed, and never good enough."

Brown has found that acknowledging and speaking shame reduces its power over us. Brown states that "Shame loves secrecy. The most dangerous thing to do after a shaming experience is hide or bury our story. When we bury our story, the shame metastasizes."

I needed to admit my shame, name it, and hold it with love. That would be my mission for the next phase of my life. I quickly realized all my other practices would never really take hold until I healed this shame. I could never create the life of my dreams when I didn't believe I deserved it.

I developed a simple practice for myself during that Venus retrograde that became the path back to worthiness. I began writing love letters to myself. Each morning, after my ritual bath, I would sit down and write about the things I loved about myself. Not my achievements or my potential, but the things that really mattered—my resilience, my capacity for joy, my willingness to keep trying even when everything felt impossible. I would also write how much I loved the choices I made and was even grateful for them. I would write down all the things that brought up shame and find love for the person who lived those choices.

Some days, these letters would trigger more tears. The gap between the love I was trying to feel and the shame I actually felt seemed impossibly wide. Other days, my heart would open and believe what I was writing. Those days when my heart began to trust me again, I felt glimmers of real, unconditional love for myself—not love dependent on what I'd done or hadn't done, but love for my simple existence.

As I continued writing these letters to myself, I began to feel changes in how I perceived myself and my worthiness. The process wasn't always easy or comfortable, but it healed me.

I started seeing my failures as the things that made me. I also began separating myself from my choices. I wasn't my choices. I wasn't a failure. I had made some mistakes, but most of them came from a place of love and they certainly didn't define me.

This practice forced me to confront how conditional my self-love had always been. I could love myself when I was succeeding, when I was making "good" choices, when I was living up to expectations. But could I love myself when I had made questionable choices? When I had failed? When I had lost everything?

This was the real work: Learning to love myself not despite my mistakes but including them, understanding that every choice, even the ones I regretted, had brought me to where I needed to be in my journey. I had to love it all and love my whole self, not just the parts that looked good on paper.

As my sense of worthiness expanded, so did what I could perceive and receive. My brain's RAS, no longer programmed to filter out opportunities due to unworthiness, was now noticing the possibilities that had been there all along. I soon started receiving more invitations to teach; I had new ideas for what I could try next in my life; I even started thinking about how I might want to love again, have a family one day, and buy a home. The very first vision I set about having a "normal" life became not just a real possibility, but something I was worthy of having. Something I deserved just by being me.

When we believe we're unworthy, our brain filters out positive opportunities and connections, dismissing them as "not for me" or "must be a mistake." As my sense of self-worth strengthened, this filter began to change, allowing me to recognize and receive the abundance that had always been available to me. I felt worthy enough to build a website for my yoga practice, which brought in more clients. I started posting regularly on Instagram. I even planned a trip to Bali with girlfriends, no longer feeling the need to travel alone, but worthy of the company of others.

And from a spiritual perspective, it felt like the Universe brought me opportunities that matched my self-worth. And it did. My energy and brain had finally allowed me to recognize them. You always have exactly what you need. The Universe, your Higher Self, and your subconscious mind all work together to consistently seek out opportunities for you to manifest your visions. When you write intentions, you are programming your energy and brain to focus on these opportunities. You tune the filter and then you can continuously find ways to manifest your intentions.

When you feel worthy of those manifestations, then you allow yourself to not only find and recognize opportunities but to step into them. You resist the old patterns that may have caused you to sabotage these opportunities or even ignore them. Instead, you feel gratitude for them and you seize them. You allow yourself to manifest your dreams because you feel worthy of them.

During those predawn hours in the bath, I began reflecting on all the women I'd been. The ambitious academic, the hippie with her crystals and astrology books, the devoted partner, the spiritual student, and the teacher. Each version had served its purpose, teaching me something about who I was and who I could become. But now it was time to step into a new version—one that could hold all these past selves with compassion and respect while remaining open to whatever was next.

I found it helpful to acknowledge all the different versions of myself I'd been, rather than rejecting them. Each of these selves had protected me in some way and had valuable wisdom to share. By integrating these past versions rather than disowning them, I began to experience a sense of wholeness. I was able to step out of the rabbit hole of shame and thank these past versions for the choices they made that led me to where I wanted to be. They were all doing the best they could at the time, and I loved them all.

This wasn't about pretending my past hadn't happened or that I'd never made mistakes. It was about recognizing that each chapter of my life had contributed to who I was becoming. It was about understanding that my worth wasn't dependent on having a perfect history. It was inherent in my being, regardless of what paths I had walked.

This is what self-worth really means. Not that you're perfect or that you never make mistakes, but that you trust you can always learn and grow from whatever life brings. It means understanding that your worth isn't something you earn or lose. It's your birthright. Your worth belongs to you and no one else. And only you can take it away from yourself.

Those morning rituals gradually evolved into something more than just personal healing. As I aligned with the energy of Venus retrograde, I began to feel my connection to the Universe and all the love it holds. I felt my oneness with everything and not just the energetic connection, but a deep connection to the most powerful energy of all: love. And it was love that lead me here to where I was sitting. Love had always guided me, even when I wanted to abandon it. And that same universal love was bringing me home to my heart.

Over those forty days of Venus retrograde, I learned to love myself again, to forgive myself fully and allow myself to heal the shame that kept me from what I was ready to manifest. I also felt an immense gratitude for the life I had created and was creating.

Venus retrograde in Leo was showing me exactly what I needed to learn: how to love myself boldly and without condition, how to hug the different versions of myself that needed not just understanding but compassion, and how to let my heart know that I was ready to follow it once more. The astrological wisdom I'd studied for decades became a living map for my healing journey.

Healing is not just about getting over past hurts or learning to trust again. It's about discovering that your capacity for feeling is your greatest strength. The very sensitivity that made you vulnerable to deep pain also gives you access to powerful wisdom and connection.

The practices that helped me open my heart again might look different from what will work for you. Maybe instead of predawn baths and love letters, you need midnight walks or afternoon dance sessions or daily pages in your journal. The form doesn't matter as much as the intention: to create space for your heart to remember your worthiness. To give yourself space to lean into shame and understand it without cringing or shying away from it. Find practices that help you honor your whole self and all your past versions, giving them the unconditional love they deserve. You are not your past mistakes, and no matter how many you've made in your lifetime, you are still worthy of an amazing future. Furthermore, you can still create that future.

In the healing process what matters most is that you begin. That you trust the process. That you allow yourself to feel everything—the joy, the pain, and the shame. Feel your doubt and the grief over what is ending. Feel all that so something else can begin. Because that's what makes you amazing—not that you never get hurt or lost, but that you have the courage to keep opening, keep feeling, keep becoming.

This is your invitation to come home to yourself. To remember your worth. To honor your past and hold it with compassion and gratitude.

You are worthy of this journey. You are worthy of healing the deepest parts of your heart, so you can be free to create the life you deserve.

Chapter Seventeen
YOU CHOOSE IT ALL

They say the moon pulls at more than just the tides. It pulls at the very fabric of our energetic being, and if there is anything left to shed, the moon will find it. Just when I thought my healing journey was complete, I met the Cancer full moon. If you've ever heard me call this the most emotional moon of all, this is why.

Months after my journey with Venus retrograde, the final full moon of the year hung heavy in the sky. I felt it pull at the deepest layer of my soul, the last threads of attachment binding me to a life I needed to release. I sat cross-legged on my bedroom floor, Juno curled beside me, steam rising from my cup of tea like prayers into the darkness. The moonlight streamed into my window across my journal pages as I wrote the final letter to Chad, not to send, but to finally let him go.

It had been years since I'd seen him. I had no idea where he was or who he was with. I still felt attached to his energy, though. And I knew this attachment, however small, kept me bound to the past. I would never be able to move forward into the life I was envisioning without completely letting go of my love for him.

Even though I was healing in powerful ways, he would still pop up in my mind. I'd wonder where he was, what he was doing, if he'd been found. Did he still love me, did he ever love me? These weren't daily questions, but still questions that plagued me at times, and I knew they were blocking my path forward. My energy was still attached to him, like a thread that I needed to cut. The Cancer full moon was my opportunity to cut that thread once and for all.

Over the past months, I'd begun creating my own lunar rituals, finding rhythm in the moon's cycles that matched the ebb and flow of healing. Each new moon became an opportunity to check in with myself about what I wanted and where I was headed. I wrote detailed intentions and felt the next vision of my life emerging.

Each full moon was an invitation to release whatever I felt was blocking me from the intentions set on the new moon. There were always blocks and there was always more to release. But this Cancer full moon felt different. It carried the energy of completion, as if maybe, just maybe, I could release enough to feel that there was no more to release.

The letter flowed easily and so did the tears of release. I wrote years of unspoken words, allowing them to finally be felt and seen. I wrote about the love we'd shared, the heartache it caused, the fear it created. I wrote about what I did wrong and what he did wrong. I wrote about forgiveness—not just for him, but for myself. I wrote about how I stayed too long, how I should have left sooner, how I wasn't strong enough back then. I wrote about how I lost myself in his chaos and how I blamed him when really I was the one to blame. I wrote about how I was ready to release the belief that love meant sacrifice and how I wanted to change that. Most importantly, I wished him well and let him know his energy was no longer welcome in my life. I was ready to be free of him and I was ready to love again.

As the words poured out, I felt something finally release. Held in the space of the Cancer full moon, I let go of every last drop of pain that I had ever felt about my relationship with Chad. I cut the cord.

When the last word was written, I knew what to do. I set up a small ritual space: a white candle, a cauldron, and the morganite crystal I had laid on my heart during countless nights of tears. That crystal energetically healed me in ways I couldn't heal myself.

I looked at the letter, taking in all the words at once, and then with a deep exhale said, "Thank you," bringing the paper to the fire, "and goodbye." I watched the paper catch fire and quickly threw it in the cauldron, where it would turn to ash. I would later bring it and my morganite to the ocean, to throw the ashes into the waves and cleanse my morganite under the light of the full moon.

As the paper burned, I envisioned my pain being transformed into pure energy, ready for the Universe to make it into something else. Everything is energy, after all. Even heartbreak can be transformed into something beautiful, because underneath the pain is the beauty of love. I knew my pain would become love once again.

That release was brought on by an intention I had set two weeks earlier. That's the thing about intentions: You set them, then you get shown what you need to release to manifest them. Through my intentions, under the new moon, I called in this release, even though I didn't know it. I wrote intentions, calling in the love I now knew I deserved. But in order to manifest that love, I had to walk through this final process of release with the Cancer full moon.

Looking back now, I can see how each step of my journey had been preparing me for this choice. I chose to let go of my pain. I chose to release the final attachment I had to my past. I chose because I knew if I didn't, I would never be able to choose my future. I wouldn't be able to choose myself.

Every challenge, every heartbreak, every moment of uncertainty had been teaching me that while we can't always control what happens to us, we always have the power to choose our lives. We choose what we're willing to carry forward and what we need to let go.

The monthly moon rituals I'd been developing became practical tools for choosing and manifesting my life. They were frameworks for rewiring my brain. They kept me on a rhythm that supported monthly check-ins with my intuition and helped me understand what I needed to release to really begin manifesting my life. I was starting to believe I had the power to change my life, and the moon became my best friend in this process.

This period in my life became the foundation of what would later grow into the Spirit Daughter workbooks, the guided journal I write each month, designed to help others connect with the power of the lunar cycles and their own spiritual journey through rituals and practices. Although I didn't know it yet, one day I would be ready to share the magic I was experiencing each new and full moon with millions of people.

The sharing of my moon rituals started simply. One evening, my roommate, Stella, walked into my room, curious about new moon rituals. Something about her question lit me up. All the wisdom I'd gathered through years of studying consciousness and energy wanted to pour out. We began meeting monthly, creating intentions under the dark moon, watching as the Universe responded with precision to our clearly stated desires.

The process taught me something powerful about manifestation. It's not about controlling outcomes but about feeling the life we truly desire. This is where intuition helps us; it leads us to understand what our soul and hearts really want. From this place of alignment, we can feel our vision. We can feel what it would be like to truly live it. Then from this feeling, we can expand, we can relax into the space of possibility, and we can manifest from knowing, not from control, fear, or anxiety.

When I first started writing intentions on the new moon, they were tentative questions more than declarations. I didn't know who I was or what kind of life I wanted to create. But the practice itself became my teacher. Each month, as I put pen to paper, I discovered pieces of myself I'd forgotten or never knew existed. The intentions helped illuminate my true desires from beneath layers of fear and old stories. Through this process of writing and witnessing what unfolded, I slowly remembered who I was and what I wanted.

Once I did the work to heal myself, my shame, and my heartache, I stopped doubting myself. I committed to every intention as if it was already real.

My divorce from Chad was long final when I wrote the vision of my future husband under the Sagittarius new moon in December 2015, so it came from a place of wholeness rather than need. I was very specific about the type of partner I wanted in my life, and I believed with my whole heart that I deserved and was worthy of this type of love and partner. I wrote about how I would feel around him. I wrote about how I would make him feel. I wrote that he would be the type of person who paid taxes, and I wouldn't feel the need to hide or lie to him. I could feel the honesty and openness in our relationship. I could feel the respect and the mutual appreciation. I could feel a different kind of love waiting for me, one that could lead to a marriage and sounds of young children. I could even feel what was required to build a relationship like this, and I called in someone who would be willing to show up and do the work with me—not when it was easy but when it got challenging.

I wrote so many things in that single vision, and I believed all of them. I believed this person existed. I believed I deserved them, and I believed I would find them, or they would find me.

I met Garrett a month later, at a friend's party, a friend whom I had met through Michael when I was couch surfing. A seed had been planted years ago, and I hadn't even known it.

Standing in a room full of people, I saw what appeared to be a light shining directly on a man and I instantly knew I had to talk to him. Meeting Garrett felt like meeting an old friend, like someone I had known from college or even earlier. Perhaps I had written my intentions with such precision, my brain immediately recognized him as familiar when I talked to him. He was my intention in tangible form, exactly. Almost a decade later, Stella, who I wrote the intention with on the new moon, still tells people how I manifested my husband on a new moon with mind-blowing precision.

What was even more incredible was that I had become a woman who was attracted to a healthy relationship. I had healed and meeting Garrett was proof of it. The old me wouldn't have even noticed him in the room, I would have filtered him out. I was now someone who could be attracted to stability rather than chaos, and that felt amazing. More than amazing, it felt whole. I felt whole and I felt healed.

My final confirmation that Garrett was the one came when I asked him his birthday—August 17. I've had four best friends throughout my life, starting at the age of four, with that same birthday. I had just manifested my next best friend.

We've been together ever since and live in a California bungalow in Venice Beach with our two children. I look at our family every day and remind myself of the power of intentions, the power of believing in myself, and my power to create the life I desire.

This is what awakening to your power really means—recognizing that you have the power to change, to heal, to create a life, and to find new versions of yourself. You are never stuck, you are never without hope. You can always, always find a way forward. You can always save yourself and choose a life that brings you joy and love and makes you feel whole.

The lunar cycles provide a natural framework for what I found to be an evolution of choice and power. New moons are times for visioning and planting seeds of intention. Full moons offer opportunities for release and celebration. The steady rhythm of waxing and waning remind us that all of life moves in cycles, that periods of growth naturally alternate with periods of rest, that release creates space for renewal.

Awakening to your power, though, isn't just about following the moon's phases or writing intentions in journals. It is about fully embodying the understanding that we choose it all—our responses, our perspectives, our next steps. When challenges arise, we choose whether to see them as obstacles or opportunities. When doors close, we choose whether to bang against them or look for windows opening elsewhere.

We also have the power to choose how we respond to familiar patterns. The power to find meaning in madness, to create beauty from chaos, to transform pain into purpose. This is the power that can never be taken from you, because it lives in the space between stimulus and response, in that pause where choice lives.

Through my studies and personal experience, I came to understand how trauma affects our ability to choose, how it can shrink that precious space between what happens to us and how we react. When we're triggered or afraid, this space becomes so small it's almost nonexistent. In that compressed moment, our nervous system hijacks our response. We fight, flee, or freeze before our conscious mind even registers what's happening. We become prisoners of our patterns, reacting from old wounds rather than responding from present wisdom.

The space between stimulus and response isn't fixed. It's elastic.

Through healing, we can stretch it, expand it, make it wide enough to breathe in. Wide enough to notice what's happening in our body. Wide enough to feel the familiar pull of an old pattern and choose differently.

This expansion of space is where our power lives. It's the difference between being controlled by our past and consciously creating our future. When someone says something that would have once sent me spiraling, I now have room, maybe just a few seconds at first, but that's enough to pause. To notice the heat rising in my chest, the tension in my jaw. To take a breath. To ask myself: "How do I want to respond? Who do I want to be in this moment?"

Each time I caught myself before reacting automatically, whether to a difficult email or an unexpected challenge, I was rebuilding my ability to choose. I was training my nervous system that we have options beyond our old survival strategies. That pause became my doorway to change. In that space, I could step out of fight-or-flight and into possibility. I could respond from my power instead of my pain. I could become someone new, one conscious choice at a time.

I also was able to choose how I saw or perceived circumstances in my life. I was able to reframe situations in ways that worked for me, not against me. I could change my reaction to someone saying no to me, for instance, seeing it as a reroute to something better and not as proof of my unworthiness. I could choose my reaction, and in that choice, I could change my perception and my energy. I could choose how I would react, and that choice became my power.

This is what makes you truly amazing—not that you never face difficulties, but that you have the power to transform them into stepping stones.

Not that you never feel fear, but that you can choose to act with courage anyway.

Not that you never get lost, but that you can always choose to begin again, to realign with your truth, to remember your inherent worthiness of all you desire.

The realization of your power to choose everything in your life changes everything. You have the power to create your life, and you have the power to change your responses. You have the power to rewire your nervous system, and you have the power to teach your brain to step out of its comfort zone and accept a new, unknown reality.

I realized much of this through working with the lunar cycles. I remembered I was in control of my life, and I was always in a constant cocreation with the Universe, which I always was part of.

What I didn't understand at first, but came to learn through experience, was how deeply these new moon intentions were working with my own brain. For years, I had stayed in situations that felt familiar even when they weren't healthy, like being with someone who lived outside the law or choosing uncertainty over stability. My brain had learned to interpret these situations as "safe" simply because they were known.

But every time I sat down under the dark moon to write intentions, I was teaching my nervous system to recognize a new kind of safety. As I wrote about the stable, loving partnership I desired, as I imagined myself thriving in a different kind of life, I was creating new neural pathways. Each intention became a bridge between my current reality and the one I was calling in.

The monthly practice of sitting with these visions, feeling them as if they were already real, began to transform something deep within me. I was rewiring my own acceptance of what was possible for my life. I was learning to feel safe with stability, to trust that I could have love without drama, to believe that I deserved a life that didn't require constant vigilance.

This understanding of how our brains cling to the familiar began to illuminate other patterns in my life. For years, I had lived like a nomad, never fully settling anywhere, always ready to pack up and leave at a moment's notice. Even after the federal agents stopped watching me, even after Chad was long gone, I continued to live with one foot out the door. My brain had learned to interpret this state of constant readiness as safety.

When I started writing intentions about creating a healthy relationship for myself, I noticed immediate resistance. My body would tense at the thought of genuine commitment, my mind would spin scenarios about why it wasn't the right time. My brain was fighting to keep me in familiar territory, even though that territory no longer served me.

So, I began to work with this resistance deliberately during my moon practices. Under each full moon, I would write about not just what I wanted to create, but how it would feel to fully inhabit that reality. I imagined what it would be like to let my guard down and share vulnerable truths, to plan a future with someone, and to create a love and a life that didn't require an escape route.

With each intention I wrote, with each vision I allowed myself to feel fully, I was rewiring my neural pathways to accept a new kind of reality. Intentions helped me change my internal landscape, teaching my nervous system to feel safe with intimacy, stability, and being truly seen.

The power to create an intentional life lives within each of us, waiting to be remembered. Some find it on their meditation cushion, letting their breath guide them to deeper knowing. Others discover it through movement, art, or time in nature. The path matters less than the willingness to walk it, to believe in possibilities beyond what your past has shown you.

What matters most is that you recognize your power to create. You choose your life. Whether you choose to work with the moon's cycles like I did or to create your own daily practice of intention and release, know that you have everything you need within you to create the life you desire.

You don't have to follow anyone else's formula but your own. Your intuition knows exactly what you need to create the life your soul wants to live. The moon helped me remember my power, but your path might look completely different. Trust that. Trust yourself.

You are, after all, made of the same stardust that creates universes. You carry within you the same force that moves planets and grows forests from tiny seeds. Your power to create isn't something you need to earn or learn, it's something you need to remember. Something you need to create space to feel.

The life you dream of isn't too big, too ambitious, or too far away. It's waiting for you to align with it. It's waiting for you to open yourself to receiving it. It's waiting for you to trust that you're worthy of it. Because you are. You are that amazing. You are that powerful. You are that worthy.

Your only task is to remember this truth, to align with it so deeply that your nervous system recognizes it as familiar, as safe, as home. And to be grateful for it all.

There is always gratitude woven into releases. I learned to thank each experience for its lessons, each pattern for how it had once protected me, each person for the role they had played in my story. This gratitude helped my nervous system understand that letting go didn't mean losing, it meant making space for something new.

What will you choose? What story will you write? What meaning will you give to your experiences? The power is yours. It always has been. Perhaps it's time to remember that, to step fully into your role as the creator of your life, to awaken to the amazing truth that you choose it all.

Chapter Eighteen
YOU CAN HAVE IT ALL

This is where many stories of spiritual journeys end—at the moment of overcoming trauma. But that's not where the real magic happens. The true power emerges when you take everything you've learned through adversity and transform it into something that serves others. When you turn your wounds into wisdom, your pain into purpose.

Everything that broke you open can become the source of your greatest power. Every heartbreak, every betrayal, every moment you thought would destroy you but didn't—it's all preparation for something bigger than you can imagine. I know this because I've lived it. The same federal agents who once made me tremble with fear became my teachers in resilience. The friend who betrayed me taught me the power of forgiveness. The losses that shattered my world taught me how to rebuild myself stronger.

When I started Spirit Daughter, I had nothing but my intuition and a laptop. I was teaching yoga, living in a tiny apartment, still carrying the shadows of my past. But I had something more valuable than credentials or capital. I had an unshakable trust in my inner knowing. The same intuition that had guided me through federal investigations, through heartbreak, through rebuilding my life piece by piece was now telling me to use what I had learned to inspire others.

I wanted to write a book—this book actually. I wanted to tell my story to help others find their way out of darkness. But I couldn't bring myself to write the stories of pain I had endured. The wounds were too fresh, and the lessons were still integrating.

One day, I was having lunch with a friend and exclaimed that I wanted to write a book about my life. I felt I could help people with my story. Something like a self-help memoir. She laughed at my outburst and suggested I start a little smaller. Perhaps a blog would be more suitable at this time. I wasn't much of a blogger, but maybe an Instagram account would do. That day I claimed the handle @spiritdaughter.

From the first post, something clicked into place. It felt right. It felt aligned. It felt steady, unlike anything I had ever done with my life. I knew this would turn into something bigger than I could envision at the time. And even though I had no idea what that would be, I trusted that feeling of alignment.

I began sharing daily insights, weaving together astrology, spirituality, and the hard-earned wisdom of my journey. The quotes I write and the stories I tell come from my life. I learned them all through direct experience before I ever shared them with others.

When I began Spirit Daughter I didn't have a business plan. I didn't do market research. I simply shared what I knew to be true, what I wished someone had told me during my darkest moments. And people responded—not just to the information, I think, but to the realness of it all. I wasn't trying to impress anyone, I was just sharing what I knew.

Spirit Daughter grew organically, guided not by spreadsheets but by intuition. When it was time to create products, I listened to what my community needed. When it was time to hire help, I trusted the energy of the people I met. I plan through intention-setting and practice every manifestation method I teach. Every major decision in my business comes from understanding the power of my mind and my ability to direct my energy. And through the deep inner knowing and trust that through it all I found my purpose.

Spirit Daughter is proof of the power to create any reality you can imagine. It's a reflection of trusting my intuition completely. It's a process of understanding that every challenge is actually an initiation. And it's my proof that my real power lies in my ability to believe in myself. That's when magic happens.

I remember the first time I truly felt this power. I was standing in my new office, not borrowed space, not a corner of someone else's business, but my own. Sun was pouring through the windows, catching the crystals on my shelves at just the right angle, the same ones packed away all those years, creating rainbows on the walls. In that moment, I felt something. It wasn't pride exactly, but a deep recognition of my own ability to create something powerful, something meaningful, something that was my soul. I had built this, not just the business, but this new version of myself.

And like I said in the very beginning, I'm not special by any means. I am no different than you. You too can create anything you desire. Whether it's a thriving business, a family, or a trip around the world, you can create it. You are not defined by what's happened to you or limited by where you've been. You are in a constant state of becoming, and at any moment, you can choose to become something new. You can save yourself and claim the life you want to live.

And yes, there will be moments of doubt. That's called being human. There will be moments when you temporarily forget or lose a connection with your power. This happens to all of us. Even now, years into running a successful business, there are moments when I catch myself slipping back into old patterns of fear or unworthiness.

This happened to me when I was about to launch our new app, Moment. Despite years of successful launches, despite a community of millions who trust my work, I felt that familiar self-doubt and anxiety in my body. That voice that whispers "Who do you think you are?" started getting louder. I recognized the pattern. This was my old self, the one who didn't believe I was worthy of giving my gifts to the world.

These moments of forgetting are actually opportunities to remember who you are. When doubt appears, treat it like an old friend just visiting for the afternoon. Acknowledge its presence, but don't let it move in. Remember that doubt is just a thought, not a truth. Your truth lives deeper than any temporary fear.

I've developed specific practices for these moments of forgetting. First, I pause whatever I'm doing and take three deep breaths—the same breathing technique that got me through federal investigations works for a moment of self-doubt. Then I place my hand on my heart and speak to the part of myself that feels scared. The part that wants to protect me from pain by infusing doubt into my world. I say: "I see you're scared. That's okay. I know you've helped in the past and I'm here with you. But remember who you are. Remember what you've overcome. Remember your amazingness."

Sometimes the forgetting goes deeper. Sometimes it's not just a moment of doubt but a period of disconnection from your own power. During these times, it's essential to have a toolbox of practices that can help you remember:

RETURN TO YOUR BODY. Fear and doubt live in the mind, but truth lives in the body. Move your body in whatever way feels natural—dance, yoga, walking. Let your body remind you of your strength.

CONNECT WITH NATURE. For me, that means taking a walk to the ocean or spending time on the water. The ocean always brings me back to my power. Nature is just another version of ourselves. Connect with elements that reflect your inner power when you begin to doubt yourself.

REVIEW YOUR JOURNEY. Keep a "victory log"—a record of every challenge you've overcome, every intuitive hit that proved correct, every time you surprised yourself with your own strength. Read it when you need reminding.

REACH OUT TO YOUR SOUL FAMILY. Surround yourself with people who see your light, especially when you've temporarily forgotten it. I have a small circle of friends who know my whole story—when I doubt myself, they remind me of who I really am.

CREATE SOMETHING. ANYTHING. The act of creating, no matter how small, reminds us of our power to bring something new into the world. It also blocks anxious thoughts from taking over. Anxiety immediately disconnects us from our power.

The key to maintaining everything you've manifested is to build daily practices that keep you connected to your own amazingness. Rituals are the key to returning to your power over and over again. For me, this means maintaining my morning meditation practice, even (especially) when business is booming. It means taking time to journal, to move my body, and to practice gratitude. These are the foundations of my life.

Living with what you've manifested requires a different skill set than creating it. When I first built Spirit Daughter, I thought the hard part was over. What I discovered was that maintaining the energy of success brings its own challenges. It's one thing to manifest something new, it's another thing to keep up your energy and vibration to continually nurture that vision as it evolves and shifts.

Here are some tips I've learned about maintaining your manifestations:

KEEP YOUR BOUNDARIES. Success often brings more people, opportunities, and demands into your life. Learn to say no to anything that isn't a resounding yes, even if it looks good on paper.

STAY CONNECTED TO YOUR WHY. When you're successful, it's easy to get caught up in the logistics of success and even wanting more. Never lose touch with the deeper purpose that drove you to create it in the first place.

KEEP GROWING. Success can make us comfortable, and comfort can make us stagnant. Always be looking for the next level of your evolution, not out of dissatisfaction but out of a commitment to growth.

PRACTICE GRATITUDE. Every morning, I take time to appreciate everything I've created—not from a place of fear that it might disappear, but from genuine gratitude for its presence in my life.

TRUST CYCLES. Everything in life moves in cycles. There will be periods of expansion and contraction, high energy and low energy. Trust these cycles rather than fighting them and learn to move with them, not against them.

One of the biggest challenges of success, I've found, is learning to enjoy it without constantly fearing its loss. This is what Brené Brown calls "foreboding joy," that tendency to brace for disaster just when things are going well. I felt this deeply after Spirit Daughter began to take off. Part of me was waiting for everything to crumble.

This is where gratitude becomes even more important. When I find myself spiraling into fear about losing what I've built, I pause and focus on my breath, that same breath that has been with me my whole life, and I practice real gratitude for everything I have. I feel the frequency of gratitude running through me and appreciate everything I have created in my life, including my business, my marriage, and my two beautiful children. I created them all and I thank myself for putting in the work to bring all these energies into form. I also thank myself for showing up even on the days I feel imperfect or lose touch with my power. Then I carry that gratitude with me everywhere I go, letting it open my heart and allow me to continue manifesting everything I need for this journey of my life.

In moments of doubt, fear, or stagnation, remember that you are the creator of your life. Being the creator isn't about controlling every circumstance or manifesting parking spots (though that can happen). It's about something much deeper. It's about knowing, with unshakable certainty, that you have the power to write, rewrite, delete, and edit your own story.

When you fully step into being the creator of your life, you start seeing and feeling your power. You understand you choose it all and you create it all. The only thing holding you back is yourself. And one day you'll realize that everything you've endured in this life has led you to embracing your power and your bigger why.

I remember the exact moment this shift happened for me. I was sitting in my new office, surrounded by vision boards and product samples, when a notification popped up on my phone, someone sharing how my work had changed their life. In that moment, I realized that everything I'd been through hadn't happened *to* me, they had happened *for* me. They were all part of the story I needed to live to become who I am today and to help others become who they are meant to be.

When you step fully into your power as a creator, you understand that you may not be able to control everything that happens, but you can trust your ability to handle whatever comes. You understand that there will always be challenges, including more puzzles to solve, and you will know how to move through them with motivation and ease. You also know that even if you lose something or everything, you will always have your wisdom to begin again and your intuition to guide you.

You'll also be ready to take full responsibility for your energy, your choices, and your responses to life's events. You'll know that even when things happen beyond your reach you can choose how you react to them and what meaning you find in them. You can choose how you see everything in your life. That is one of your powers.

And when you actually start to believe in your power to create your life, you start to see evidence of your power everywhere. You notice the synchronicities that appear just when you need them. You notice open doors where you thought there were none. You recognize how challenges that once would have destroyed you now strengthen you. You find yourself coming up with new ideas, new inspiration, and new plans just when you need them. And the more you believe in yourself and tell yourself that through affirmations and mantras, the more your brain cocreates with the Universe to find more and more evidence of your power.

The most beautiful part about owning your power as the creator of your life is falling in love with the journey of becoming. You are constantly becoming another version of yourself and that journey, like the butterfly finding its wings after an immense struggle to freedom, is beautiful. It's not just beautiful, it's inspiring. It's amazing.

You can have it all. Life is not a series of either/or. You can create a successful career or business *and* have a family who you get to spend time with every day. You can inspire others *and* have time for self-care to fill yourself up. You can be an amazing partner *and* nourish your soul's path. You don't have to limit yourself in any way. You can have whatever life you choose. It's up to you.

So dream big. Bigger than that. Bigger still. Whatever you can imagine for your life, double it. Triple it. Then trust that the same power that brought you through every challenge so far will help you create it. Trust that amazingness is your natural state. Get up every day, look yourself in the mirror, and say, "I can do this because I am amazing," and one day, trust me, you'll start to believe it. And that will be the day your life changes.

This is your invitation to step fully into your power. To trust your intuition completely. To create whatever reality you can imagine. To remember, again and again, that you are amazing.

The power is yours. It always has been. Now go use it.

ACKNOWLEDGMENTS

To Shannon Welch, my editor, who helped me believe this book was good enough to share with the world. Your faith in this story gave me the confidence to keep going.

To Margaret Riley King, my literary agent, who challenged me from the beginning to "go deep and leave nothing for the swim home." Your push to dig deeper made this book what it is.

To my mom, Michele, who has become a great friend and an amazing grandmother. Reading parts of this book to her freed my writer's block and also healed an emotional one. Thank you for listening and for the healing that came through sharing these words with you.

To my team at Spirit Daughter, who supported my many "writing weeks" by keeping the business running without me. Your dedication allowed me the space and peace of mind to focus on this story.

To my best friend, Lia, who was with me every step of the way, cheering me on and believing in me. You lived this story with me and knew it needed to be told. Thank you for never letting me doubt that.

And to my husband, Garrett, my greatest manifestation yet. You are living proof that intentions set with a healed heart create miracles. Thank you for holding space for this story to be told, for solo parenting on countless weekends while I wrote these words, and for being the solid ground I once only dreamed of. You are everything I wrote on those new moon pages come to life.

ABOUT THE AUTHOR

JILL WINTERSTEEN is the founder of Spirit Daughter, a transformative platform that has helped millions design their best possible lives through the wisdom of astrology and conscious manifestation. Since 2016, her platform has grown to reach 2.4 million followers on Instagram, drawn to her insightful astrological guidance, cosmic wisdom, and unique blend of neuroscience and mindfulness practices.

With a master's degree in psychology and a background as a neuroscience researcher, Jill brings a unique perspective to the world of astrology and manifestation. She left her traditional academic path when her calling to help others find grounding and transformation became undeniable, trading research labs for the beaches of Venice, California, where she built a thriving practice combining alignment-based yoga, Chinese medicine, and astrological counseling. Inspired by her teaching and world travels, she decided to start Spirit Daughter, which has allowed her to reach people across the globe with her wisdom.

Through Spirit Daughter, Jill has created powerful tools for personal growth, including the Moment app, which guides users through daily mindfulness and manifestation practices aligned with astrological transits, and her popular lunar cycle workbooks, which help thousands worldwide harness the power of moon phases each month. Her Call It In Method synthesizes years of study in both New Age philosophy and

Western neuroscience, teaching students to break through limiting beliefs and create the life they desire.

Jill's work empowers her community to believe in themselves, follow their intuition, and understand that they have the power to change their lives. She currently lives in Venice Beach, with her husband, two children, and dog, Juno. She's grateful every day for the people she has found and the ones who have found her.

Avid Reader Press, an imprint of Simon & Schuster, is built on the idea that the most rewarding publishing has three common denominators: great books, published with intense focus, in true partnership. Thank you to the Avid Reader Press colleagues who collaborated on *Spirit Daughter*, as well as to the hundreds of professionals in the Simon & Schuster advertising, audio, communications, design, ebook, finance, human resources, legal, marketing, operations, production, sales, supply chain, subsidiary rights, and warehouse departments whose invaluable support and expertise benefit every one of our titles.

Editorial
Shannon Welch, *VP and Editorial Director*
Megan Noes, *Editorial Assistant*

Jacket Design
Alison Forner, *Senior Art Director*
Clay Smith, *Senior Designer*
Sydney Newman, *Art Associate*

Marketing
Meredith Vilarello, *VP and Associate Publisher*
Caroline McGregor, *Marketing Manager*
Nicholas Rooney, *Marketing Manager*
Emily Lewis, *Marketing Manager*
Katya Wiegmann, *Marketing and Publishing Assistant*

Production
Allison Green, *Managing Editor*
Hana Handzija, *Managing Editorial Assistant*
Jessica Chin, *Senior Manager of Copyediting*
Fausto Bozza, *Production Manager*
Milly McKinnish, *Interior Text Designer*
Erika R. Genova, *Desktop Compositor*
Cait Lamborne, *Ebook Developer*

Publicity
David Kass, *Senior Director of Publicity*
Alexandra Primiani, *Associate Director of Publicity*
Rhina Garcia, *Publicist*
Eva Kerins, *Publicity Assistant*

Subsidiary Rights
Paul O'Halloran, *VP and Director of Subsidiary Rights*
Rachel Podmajersky, *Subsidiary Rights Manager*
Fiona Sharp, *Subsidiary Rights Coordinator*